Fully Consecrated

Fully Consecrated

THE JOURNEY OF GOD'S FAITHFULNESS THROUGH UNDENIABLY HIS

Haley Wade

Fully Consecrated

© 2019 by Haley Wade

All rights reserved. No portion of this book may be reproduced, stored in a retrieval system, or transmitted in any form or by any means— electronic, mechanical, photocopying, recording, or other— except for brief quotations in critical reviews or articles, without the prior written permission of the author.

ISBN-13: 978-0-578-46699-6

Front cover illustration by Remington Wade. Used by permission.
Author photo by Matthew Edwards

THE HOLY BIBLE, NEW INTERNATIONAL VERSION®, NIV® Copyright © 1973, 1978, 1984, 2011 by Biblica, Inc.® Used by permission. All rights reserved worldwide.

Scripture quotations labeled KJV are from the King James Version of the Bible.

The Christian Standard Bible. Copyright © 2017 by Holman Bible Publishers. Used by permission. Christian Standard Bible®, and CSB® are federally registered trademarks of Holman Bible Publishers, all rights reserved.

Scripture quotations marked NLT are taken from the Holy Bible, New Living Translation, copyright © 1996, 2004, 2015 by Tyndale House Foundation. Used by permission of Tyndale House Publishers, Inc., Carol Stream, Illinois 60188. All rights reserved.

IN HONOR OF

MY GRANDMA DOTTY

While Dotty Vandiford Wade entered her eternal home in Heaven before I was born, my parents always told me about her. Her legacy has inspired me to invest my life in impacting others for the kingdom of God. My Grandma Dotty was a Sunday school teacher at Mount Calvary Free Will Baptist Church every week. She loved children. My DaDa did not put her confidence in material possessions. She was humble and generous with food, kind words of encouragement, and God's love. My grandma also helped run her family's store called AE Vandiford Grocery and Grill.

While growing up, DaDa helped raise her five younger siblings. She went to the Free Will Baptist Bible College in Nashville, Tennessee, and later married my granddad, Billy Ray Wade. She was the best mom she could be to my dad and his two sisters. DaDa instilled values of hard work and modesty into them.

My Grandma Dotty lived a life fully consecrated to Jesus Christ. Her hope was not in this world. No, my friend, my grandma's confidence and hope was in the love of our Lord Jesus Christ. I believe my grandma made the most of her everyday opportunities to impact people. She always had food at her table and invited others into her home no matter what state it was in. She lived in a way that reflected Jesus purely. My grandma's testimony and passion for Jesus was undeniable. She found favor among those who met her, and she persevered even when battling breast cancer. While Jesus did not intend for my grandma's life on earth to extend into old age, He helped her be intentional with every moment she had. I know Heaven will be more full because of the life my grandma lived on earth.

I am dedicating this book to Dotty Vandiford Wade as she has been one of my biggest inspirations in life. I know that although she is not living on earth anymore, her prayers are still being answered. I would not be where I am at today without the example and life that my DaDa lived.

Who are we going to impact with our everyday lives? Let's make Heaven more full because of our lives on earth.

Content

INTRODUCTION 15

2015

1. **LOVED AND PURSUED BY THE CREATOR** 19
2. **LIVE THE LIFE HE DIED FOR** 21
3. **UNIQUE** 23
4. **DON'T GIVE UP** 24
5. **HE MAKES ME BRAVE** 25
6. **LOVING DEEPLY** 26
7. **BALANCED LIFESTYLE** 27

8. **CHALLENGED SACRIFICE** 29

9. **OCTOBER LESSONS** 30

10. **LOVE IN A NEW PERSPECTIVE** 32

11. **ETERNAL BLESSINGS > SHORT JOYS ON EARTH** 34

12. **KNOW HIM PERSONALLY** 36

13. **LOCAL BEFORE GLOBAL** 38

14. **BEING HIS** 40

15. **GOALS FOR THE NEW YEAR** 43

… 2016 …

16. **BUT SEEK FIRST** … 46

17. **RESTORED BY LOVE** … 47

18. **LIVE ABUNDANTLY** … 49

19. **REMAIN IN HIM** … 51

20. **A WELL-WATERED POST** … 53

21. **ETERNAL ENCOURAGEMENT & GOOD HOPE** … 54

22. **MY YTI EXPERIENCE** … 56

23. **A MUST READ: TIPS FOR BACK TO SCHOOL** … 60

24. **BEING > DOING** … 64

25. **THE THINGS UNSEEN** … 66

26. **NOTES TO SELF:** … 68

27. **YOUR INHERITANCE** … 70

28. **TRIALS & TESTING** … 73

29. **GOD HAS ALREADY WON** 76

30. **NEVER TIRE** 77

31. **WHERE YOUR HEART IS** 79

32. **10 THINGS I LEARNED IN 2016** 81

2017

33. **I AM A CHILD OF GOD** 85

34. **MORE IN STORE** 87

35. **BE ROOTED** 89

36. **EYES ON HIM** 90

37. **16 YEARS OF LIFE** 93

38. **DURING THE JOURNEY** 95

39. **TO THE ONE WHO QUESTIONS THEIR GIFTS** 97

40. **CRIES IN THE DESERT** 99

41. **JUST STOP** 101

42. **GIVING OUR BEST** 103

43. **BUGS & NUDGES** 105

44. **CHOOSING WHAT IS BETTER** 107

45. **THE GAME OF LIFE** 110

46. **FORWARD CONFERENCE 2017** 112

47. **BORN TO STAND OUT** 117

48. **HOW TO FIND YOUR GIFTS** 119

49. **YOUNG AND BEARDLESS** 121

50. **BE STILL AND KNOW** 123

51. **KNOW WHO YOU'RE FIGHTING** 126

52. **THE 40 DAY PRAYER CHALLENGE** 128

53. **THE BACKSTORY OF MY WEEKEND AT LIBERTY** 129

54. **THE UNASHAMED PROJECT SCHOLARSHIP** 133

55. **LEAVING COMFORT** 137

56. **FIGHTING FEAR** 139

57. **LIVE ORIGINAL TOUR 2017** 143

58. **FRESHNESS OVER FAMILIARITY** 145

59. **IN CHRIST ALONE** 148

60. **RAW ENCOUNTERS** 150

61. **BE** 153

62. **THE BEST OF 2017** 155

2018

63. **LOVE IS PATIENT** 162

64. **SEVENTEEN** 165

65. **PLANTED IN FAITH** 168

66. **THE DELIGHT MOVEMENT 2018** 170

67. **FIVE TRUTHS I WAS REMINDED OF WHILE BEING WITHOUT MY CAR** 175

68. **NEW BEGINNINGS** 179

69. **THE WAY THAT YOU ARE LIVING MATTERS** 182

70. **THE DRY SEASON IS OVER** 185

71. **TRUSTING GOD IN THE UNSEEN** 190

72. **REVISITING THE CAVE** 194

73. **THRIVING THROUGH TRANSITIONS** 198

74. **IMMEASURABLY MORE** 201

75. **DOUBT DOESN'T COME FROM GOD** 205

76. **ONE GOOD STEP AT A TIME** 209

77. **2018: A FOCUS ON GOD'S FAITHFULNESS** 213

NOTES 222

ACKNOWLEDGMENTS 223

ABOUT THE AUTHOR 227

AN EXPLANATION OF THE GOSPEL 228

INTRODUCTION

I first remember writing down the words "fully consecrated" this past summer. I was in a Bible Study with some new friends and was desperately wanting God to reveal Himself to me in deeper ways. I didn't want anything in my life separating me from intimacy with my life-giving Father. I was heading into a season of many unknowns, and I was losing control of my life.

I've honestly been seeking to determine more of what "fully consecrated" means lived out. I believe God has set each of His children apart from what is average and ordinary. Our Dad gives Himself to us completely. It is a freeing thing to hand ourselves, our lives, and our deepest desires back to Him. It is a beautiful thing to be aware of the gifts God has given to each of us and seek to use all of those things to point others back to Him. Fully consecrating ourselves to the Lord is not necessarily easy. To be honest with you, it requires us pouring ourselves out before His feet. Fully consecrating ourselves to Jesus requires us to trust Him even when we cannot see where we are stepping next.

A person who is fully consecrated to Jesus Christ seeks the Lord as their highest priority. They don't allow sports, extra curricular activities, or worldly things steal their time with the Lord. A person who is fully consecrated to Jesus Christ recognizes that while they continuously bask in God's love, they can never earn it. Being fully consecrated to God takes the pressure off of us. Our lives are not inside of our hands. We are here for Jesus alone. He has a plan bigger than we can see to use our everyday moments to impact Heaven for eternity.

Being fully consecrated to Jesus isn't popular. It will result in us losing some friends. We will say "no" to things that are okay because we are saving our "yes" for His best.

A person fully consecrated to God is not living for temporary or worldly pleasures. Their eyes are on things above.

Jesus is the desire of a fully consecrated believer's heart.

A person fully consecrated to Jesus Christ doesn't waver in their loyalty to the Lord. Yes, they struggle, but they have committed their lives to the cause of Christ. They don't play church. They are the Church. Instead of claiming to be a Christian, a fully consecrated believer reflects Jesus through their actions, motives, interactions, and conversations. Their hope and identity is undeniable to anyone who encounters them.

A fully consecrated lover of God doesn't have to prove anything to those around them. They don't have to put energy into performing and seeming to be good. God flows from their lives as a result of them filling themselves up with Him.

I grew up loving Jesus, but I truly experienced His love the summer before I entered eighth grade. I felt the Holy Spirit fighting for me, pursuing me, and telling me to let go of my chaotic lifestyle. I was seeking to love the Lord, but I had distractions and idols in my life that stood in the way of my intimacy with Him.

After surrendering the things I was clinging onto, I was overwhelmed by God's perfect freedom! I lost people I was close to, but I gained the most precious Lover and Friend. My faith became my own. My relationship with Jesus was personal. I didn't just talk about God anymore. I didn't just do the minimal things in living a Christian life. No, I realized that our faith in Jesus is an every day thing. Once we taste and experience Jesus' love, we will never be the same. We won't be able to keep walking in our old ways. When our lives have been changed by Jesus Christ, we won't be able to contain the excitement and love we have for Him. Our lives will overflow in endless praise to His Name alone. We will realize that no one else is worthy of the honor that Jesus deserves. No one else loves us, pursues us, fights for us, and defends us like Jesus does.

A person who has been changed by Jesus is set apart. We don't have to question their love for the Lord. I truly believe our love for God should be undeniable. Our testimonies should show that we are not the same people we once were. We no longer walk in shame. We don't cling onto worthless things. We will only ever find our true identities in Jesus Christ. Placing our identities in outward appearances, significant others, grades, families, and friend groups does not fill us with the joy of the Lord.

There is nothing that compares to the peace that we have when we are overcome by our Father's love. We may not understand where God is taking us and what the next steps of our lives look like, but we must trust that God knows where He is taking us. We must hold on to the promises He has made. We must rest in the nudges He has deposited within us.

A person fully consecrated to the Lord will be burdened for the lost people surrounding them. They will not be satisfied with the normal life cycle. They will have God-sized dreams and visions. They will walk through wildernesses, hills, and valleys before seeing all of God's promises fulfilled. They will draw deeper into the heart of God though the process. They will be rid of themselves daily and realize that it is not about them at all.

A person fully consecrated to Jesus Christ will return to Him no matter how tired, empty, or broken they may feel.

Are you fully consecrated to our God? Will you join me in seeking His heart more than ever before?

A YEAR OF OBEDIENCE

2015

LOVED AND PURSUED BY THE CREATOR

JULY 25, 2015

Sometimes I get so focused on doing something great for God, that in the process of that, I lose sight of Him. It definitely shouldn't be this way but so easily happens.

This morning, I spent countless hours trying to figure out how to work and customize this blog. Of course, the whole purpose of it is to glorify and honor Jesus, but I wasn't even thinking of the big picture. I was more focused on what font something was, the color scheme, or if a picture was centered perfectly. We get so enraptured in little things in our daily lives to stop and think if any of it will benefit our eternities.

I walked outside to find that today is one of the most beautiful days we've had this whole summer. It's definitely beyond any creation of the Internet. There are pairs of butterflies flying around the flowers and a gentle breeze is blowing. Birds are chirping, the sun is shining, and blueberry pies are in the making. God's creation is all around us screaming His glory, but how often do we stop to appreciate it?

Today God has shown me many things. We are called to enjoy life. Jesus is our forever constant, He is always going to be God, and His love for us is always pursuing our hearts.

So today, instead of trying to take things into our own hands or spend all day on the Internet, I challenge us to go for a walk, ride our bikes, look at the clouds, or smell a flower. Let's be a little adventurous! We never know what we may find. We must allow God to show Himself to us in the ways He desires. We are loved and pursued by the Creator of the world.

LIVE THE LIFE HE DIED FOR

JULY 27, 2015

Sitting in the passenger seat of the old truck, Bryson's eyes illuminated with excitement. He was wearing his camouflage cargo pants and work boots, matching his dad. If someone told Bryson something bad about his dad, he wouldn't believe them. Bryson thought that his dad was the greatest man alive, and today he was going to work with him.

When they arrived at the job, Bryson's dad quickly got focused on how the roofing was coming along. Little Bryson got bored and wandered to the woods to find something exciting.

While Bryson was steadily walking to the woods, he started having low abdominal pains. He didn't think much of it at first but quickly realized that it could be something very serious. Before Bryson knew it, he was lying on the ground screaming for help.

Bryson's father thought he heard someone screaming. He listened closely and recognized the sound of his child. His panic stricken body was filled with worry and fear.

The next morning, Bryson woke up to a new atmosphere. Not only to a new atmosphere, but to lying in a hospital bed.

His father couldn't stand the sight of seeing his son sick and confused lying in a hospital bed. He kept blaming himself for not watching Bryson as intently as he should have.

He knew that he would do anything it took to see his son's eyes shine like they did yesterday morning.

This is a work of fiction God allowed me to write so that I can share what He is trying to say to **you**.

You are His child. When you are going through a rough time, God is going through it with you. Jesus' heart becomes grievous when He sees you wandering away from His love. We will never be able to separate or stop the love God has for us. We are His children and He is our Father.

Before the beginning of the world, God knew that you and I would be broken and need a Savior. He sent His only son, Jesus, to come and die on a cross so that we could live a life for Him on earth and have an eternity with Him in Heaven.

Like Bryson's father, we have a Father who wants to see us live life to the fullest. Jesus enjoys seeing our faces shine with His love and peace. He wants us to share what He has done in our lives and to help others see how much He loves them.

God is asking you and I, "Why would you choose to live an ordinary life whenever you have the ability and freedom in Me to live a life worthy of your calling?"

Jesus died so that you and I can live this life for Him. Will you choose to?

UNIQUE

JULY 31, 2015

I struggle with things just like we all do, but I want to use my struggles to help others. I hope you are encouraged by knowing you are not alone.

For the past couple of weeks, I have been obsessed with a certain YouTube channel. There's nothing wrong with the channel, but I made it an idol. I found myself trying to be like the youtuber and I started comparing my life to hers.

God spoke to my heart and has been convicting me about this. **When we spend countless minutes seeing how we can become like someone else, we become unhappy with the life God has given to us.** He wants us to use our time much more wisely than using it to chase after the world. He created us to be **unique.** We aren't supposed to look like people living for selfish pleasures.

Thankfully, God doesn't leave us to take on hard things alone. He offers us His loving and helping hand. We just have to reach out and grab it. Our Father knows we will fail Him so much, but He already tells us that He will give us grace and forgiveness.

Let's be more adventurous in our relationships with God. I want a "fresh fire" to stir in my heart and revive me. We never have to settle or be satisfied with where we are at in our relationships with Jesus. He desires for us to thirst for more. God has so much in store for our lives. We just have to keep pursuing Him each day. Keep your head up today and allow God to take over every aspect of your life!

DON'T GIVE UP

AUGUST 5, 2015

The devil wants nothing more than to steal our dreams and our love for God. When we go through trials, it's easy to get discouraged and think about giving up. Although that is true, we can't give in to either of those feelings. God has so much in store for us.

Galatians 6:9 (NIV) says, "Let us not become weary in doing good, for at the proper time we will reap a harvest if we do not give up."

That verse brings so much hope and motivation to my spirit. Let's meditate on it today. Let's seek Jesus and pray for strength to fight off the flesh while we also abide in His Word.

HE MAKES ME BRAVE

AUGUST 24, 2015

This past week, I was asked to speak in front of our whole church. It was something completely outside of my comfort zone. I knew that Jesus had opened the door of opportunity for me so I couldn't just close it. Through this experience, God has taught me a few lessons that I want to share with you.

1. Don't limit the ways God can use you.

We all have things we're good at and enjoy doing, but we also usually neglect what comes hard. God wants us to do more than what's easy. He wants us to exercise, and get better in every aspect of our lives so that we can give Him the glory.

2. Jesus was publicly humiliated and crucified for us.

Why aren't we more motivated to share the good news of everything God did, has done, and is doing in our lives?

3. He makes us brave.

What is holding you back from living out your purpose? Whatever it is, Jesus wants to set you free from it. He will call you out to do things you won't be able to handle on your own. With God's Strength, Presence, and Peace, we can be strong and brave!

LOVING DEEPLY

AUGUST 31, 2015

There's a person that we all have in our lives. The one who doesn't have the nicest clothes and doesn't smell or behave like we do. We could easily ignore this person, but we are called to do so much more than that.

We're called to make love a verb rather than a noun. We must spread kindness everywhere we go through our words, actions, and lives. We should also practice humility by putting other's needs before our own, not caring about being made fun of. By listening to what others have to say and by being present in their lives, we offer friendship and a caring atmosphere. **There is no greater way to lead people to the greatest Love than by showing them what Love really looks like.**

Who were you thinking about while reading this? I challenge you to look for opportunities to show them Love this week. You shine bright, my friend! Never stop loving or serving those around you!

"'The King will reply, 'Truly I tell you, whatever you did for one of the least of these brothers and sisters of mine, you did for me.'" -Matthew 25:40 (NIV)

"The second is this: 'Love your neighbor as yourself.' There is no commandment greater than these.'"-Mark 12:31 (NIV)

BALANCED LIFESTYLE

SEPTEMBER 21, 2015

Managing our agendas while also trying to spend time with the Lord daily can sometimes be a challenge. We can't stop growing in our relationships with God to study all of the time, and we can't neglect our homework to only read the Bible. We have to find a balance.

Today I want to share some tips with you on living a more balanced lifestyle. I could definitely use a post like this so I hope that you will find it helpful.

- **Prioritize**

Do you write down everything or do you prefer memorization? Either way, I think that lists are helpful. They keep us organized but also give us a game plan on how to tackle all that we need to do.

- **Be motivated and know your limits**

Make some goals. I would encourage you to write them out where you can look at them frequently. You will be motivated by knowing what you're working towards.

Whenever I read my Bible, I sometimes just flip through it and read highlights or things that catch my attention. That process usually results in a lot of passages being read but not many being understood. It's better to read less and get more rather than struggle to apply so many deep thoughts.

- **Use your time wisely**

After being at school for eight hours, I don't think diving into homework when we first get home is what most of us dream of doing. It's important that we give ourselves a little break. In doing this, we have to be careful not to waste any time. Getting started on homework and chores early will hopefully pay off whenever we're able to go to bed earlier.

- **Have a special meeting place**

This is a place where you can go and be by yourself. A place where you feel open to worship God freely and invite His Spirit to come speak to your heart. Although we all grow in different ways, I absolutely love my "walks and talks" with Jesus. My backyard is my special meeting place. I enjoy discovering more about God and His character while also enjoying His creation.

The most important thing for us to remember is that Jesus is the only One who can give us peace and rest.

"Do not be anxious about anything, but in every situation, by prayer and petition, with thanksgiving, present your requests to God. And the peace of God, which transcends all understanding, will guard your hearts and your minds in Christ Jesus." -Philippians 4:6-7 (NIV)

"Cast your cares on the Lord and he will sustain you; he will never let the righteous be shaken." -Psalm 55:22 (NIV)

CHALLENGED SACRIFICE
OCTOBER 5, 2015

Today in Bible class, my teacher asked who would stand up and proclaim that they weren't ashamed of God. None of us were expecting this and were feeling shocked, scared, and nervous. While our minds were racing, the topic changed before anyone had time to stand up.

When we hear about situations like what happened in Oregon just this past week, we want to believe that we would also make the right decision. In reality, we don't really know how we would react.

Thankfully, what happened in my Bible class was **far** from a life or death situation, but it has given me a new kind of perspective.

What kind of boldness do we have when it comes to taking a big stand for Christ?

What are we willing to give up for Him?

OCTOBER LESSONS

OCTOBER 12, 2015

God put something special on my heart a few weeks ago and I acted upon it. He answered prayer in a huge way and I had never seen Him answer a prayer that quickly.

On Friday, I started letting the devil steal my joy and fervent urgency to continue to lift up that certain situation.

I felt change wasn't happening, what I wanted wasn't coming about, and that I should just stop trying to make it happen.

The truth is that I cannot make change happen, a friendship grow, or give someone the courage that they need to go against the current of likeness. The only One who can bring about all of these things is God our Father, the Creator of Heaven and Earth.

I am called to stay in continual pursuit of God in prayer over this.

I want to share three things with you that God has been showing to me.

1. You must fill yourself up to pour yourself out.

We want to help and invest into others. In order to do that, we have to be investing into ourselves and our relationships with God. Therefore, He will be what comes out of our daily lives.

2. Don't let the devil steal your joy, purpose, or love.

The enemy is out to only kill, steal, and destroy you. When you're on fire for God, and God is using you to build His kingdom, you become a target to tear down. The devil doesn't want you to keep building up an army of Christ. Be on guard and fight your battles through prayer and quiet time with the Lord.

3. Surround yourself with people who will point you closer to Christ

God has blessed me with many new friendships this year with people who I've known but never really gotten to know deeply. Having at least one friend who has a genuine heart for Christ will make a huge impact in your life. I get so upset seeing the people who need to be encouraged the most being torn down. Show yourself friendly, and I'm sure God will send you the right friends. Just be yourself and let God shine through you. Believe me, it's more attractive than what you think.

LOVE IN A NEW PERSPECTIVE

OCTOBER 19, 2015

We grow up thinking we **have** to find someone who accepts us, looks at us with heart eyes, and wants to get married to spend life together.

I believe that God created us for such a greater purpose than seeking earthly love for ourselves.

Before we're ready for our earthly loves, we need to know where our true joy comes from.

It comes from God and having a true relationship with Him. It's seeking His heart and finding it. It's being crazy passionate about the things He has in store for our lives.

Jesus is the one to look to in times of troubles and seek through every season. **If we don't love Him with everything that we are and have, then how do we expect to love others properly?**

We need to trust that God will bring our future mates into our lives in His timing, and be reminded that true love isn't found by seeking it for ourselves.

Nothing can separate or stand in the way of the plans God has for our lives.

No matter where we go, if we're seeking God about our futures, we should trust that He will lead us.

We all have dreams and a longing for our special person. Myself included. I think that our perspectives sometimes get out of order. Because of this, I want to challenge you to not look at this time of singleness in your life as a punishment. God wants you to be more serious about your relationship with Him.

He also wants to prepare you for the things ahead. Be patient, don't settle for less, and be your future mate's biggest prayer warrior.

ETERNAL BLESSINGS> SHORT JOYS ON EARTH

NOVEMBER 2, 2015

What is your motivation (the reason or reasons one has for acting or behaving in a particular way) in life? What do you think of being worth all of your hard work each day?

I do hope your family came to mind, and they are excluded from what I'm about to talk about.

Is the most important thing in your life purchasing a new boat, gun, camera or wardrobe? Do thoughts of having the item consume your mind? Do you spend all of your energy working towards a material goal?

If you thought yes to any of those questions, then maybe God will show you all that He has to me today.

We work so hard for things that will soon fade away or be replaced. Why don't we give more of our time and energy to making a difference in other people's eternities? If we really think about it, our eternity is just that. For eternity (infinite or unending time).

Wouldn't you rather reap a harvest of blessings in Heaven for eternity rather than have short joys here (on Earth) that will soon pass away?

God doesn't give us "free days" where we aren't expected to live for Him, love Him more, and reach out to His people. **You** woke up today with **purpose.** Please do not waste your potential on short joys. Give your everything to making a difference in our world, and people's eternal souls. That's all that really matters.

KNOW HIM PERSONALLY

NOVEMBER 9, 2015

In a Christian setting, most people will claim to know Jesus, but do they really know Him personally or just Who He is?

Knowing Who Jesus is can be heard about through many different ways. Do we, as believers, display His characteristics in a positive way? Is our faith like the church of Colossae that Paul mentions in the book of Colossians?

Their faith was not just known, but also talked about between people they had never met. That's how impactful their love for God was.

Often times, we don't think about all of the situations, people, or prayers that God allowed in our lives just for the purpose of us coming to believe in Him.

Love isn't really love if it's forced, and Jesus desires to be loved freely.

There is someone I have prayed for many many times. I desire their salvation, and for them to experience true freedom and pleasure through having a personal relationship with Jesus.

Jesus whispered a message to my heart. "I want him and love him. He has to choose Me."

Jesus has done His part in making the way for our salvation. Will or have you accepted His gift? If you're struggling with doubt or confusion, please talk to someone who you trust and who has a personal relationship with God. I'm always here if you need someone to talk to also.

One of my life verses is 2 Timothy 1:7 (KJV). Let it give you peace tonight.

"For God hath not given us the spirit of fear; but of power, and of love, and of a sound mind."

Leave fear, worry, anxiety, and doubt with Jesus. He already took all of those things on Himself so you wouldn't have to. I challenge you to break down Colossians 3:12. Always remember that you're *wanted and loved.*

LOCAL BEFORE GLOBAL

NOVEMBER 23, 2015

"If you want to be a missionary to another country, how do you expect to change another part of the world if you aren't being a part of change where you are now?"

My Bible teacher said this a couple months ago and it really has stuck with me.

Recently, I've realized how broken some people actually are. Sin has ruined or is ruining their lives. They are thirsty for love, acceptance, joy, and happiness while looking everywhere but to Jesus to find it.

People care more about what their friends think of them rather than the Creator of the world. Why? I don't think many people realize how real Jesus is.

Today in Bible Study girls were honest about their struggles. We were able to pray over one of our friends who is going through a hard time. I see potential in my peers, but I also know that the devil wants to make them stumble. Each of the girls in Bible Study desire to love Jesus more, but we have to help each other and put forth personal effort. **We can't expect to get closer to God by only talking about it.**

God has given me a school, a group of girls for Bible Study, teachers in need of encouragement, children at church, my peers, family, and just people that I come in contact with each day to invest in.

God has equipped you to go out, be His disciple, show love, spread joy, and display an authentic relationship with Him. Let Him use you. I promise it will help you grow in your own walk with Him. **Investing into others is a blessing**

and seeing God work is a reward. Who are the people in your life that were specifically put in your path? How can you stand up and be a leader?

Tonight, let's pray about our influence and leadership. Don't forget your purpose.

BEING HIS

DECEMBER 7, 2015

In this time of being prepared for my future husband, God is showing me what true love really looks like.

God has shown me that when He sees us at our absolute worst, He also sees potential. He starts to reshape and purify our hearts and lives.

He desires to know us intimately which means we have to be real, honest, pure, and open. We have to cherish Him and invest into our relationships with Him **above all other things**. We also have to invest into others and devote ourselves to service, while not forgetting to sit quietly in the presence of God while He pours into us.

Jesus has shown me where my true joy comes from. I can't seek fulfillment and satisfaction in the world. Seeking the world leads to insecurity, envy, and forgetting how blessed we already are.

He has given me a distinct sense of purpose in this life, and is continually showing me that our purpose is to stand out and to be different.

Jesus is also teaching me to be **His** and how to display His love in such a real and authentic type of way. I'm called to obey without knowing all of the details, simplify life, and seek my Father first. I must also show others that they don't have to continue to live in sin while I help them find new life in Christ. I've been burdened to disciple new believers as they grow in His grace.

Jesus already knows the next thing I will struggle with or when I will spend more time doing something I desire than in quiet time with Him. In spite of this, He doesn't stop wanting, seeking, loving, or forgiving me.

God goes before us, preparing the way to make us brave when we're called to step out in faith. **Every day of quiet time, prayer or church service is preparing us for the things He has in store for our lives.**

Jesus is our Redeemer. He breaks our chains. He takes our spirits of fear, worry, and anxiety to the cross where He died so that we wouldn't have to bear them.

He helps us overcome the things that are holding us back from walking in the life of service God is calling us into.

He pierces our hearts when He knows we're struggling or when He sees someone else struggling that we need to help.

Abba opens our eyes to our spiritual gifts and starts developing them in us. He desires us to use them for His glory. He takes what we have to offer and multiplies the ways He'll be able to use them to reach His people.

Jesus teaches us patience when we are thirsty for His presence and long for special moments with Him. He shows us that when we wait, He gives us His very best.

These are just the highlights of what God has shown me. Each group of words written above is related to a season in my life.

In seventh grade, I struggled with perfection, comparison, insecurities, and my relationship with God. I was trying to live out the "perfect image" that our world promotes.

Jesus personally became my **Redeemer** that summer as He freed me from a relationship that was unhealthy. I thought that some things in my life were falling apart. I now realize that we sometimes have to go to a "broken" state before we realize Who makes us whole. I have experienced the process of being made whole.

Last year, I grew so much in my personal relationship with Jesus. I watched Him reveal and develop my spiritual gifts. I longed for His presence in my daily life and clung to Him through late and stressful nights of homework. School was hard and the devil was using spirits of fear, anxiety, and worry to torment me.

I was so scared of public speaking. My middle school pastor asked me to speak for our youth take over service the Sunday after the United Conference this summer. I was wanting to say no. Let me remind you, I was thinking that it was just going to be Sunday school. The fact that it was "big church" was another level in my mind. God wouldn't let me *not* do it though. I knew that He was opening the door of opportunity for me so I couldn't just close it. It was a leap of faith and I knew I would have to rely on *Jesus'* strength and power to do it.

While at the United Conference on that Friday night, the pastor was talking about God breaking the chains of the things holding us back from living out our purpose. My struggle was with fear. I was freed from that burden. Jesus made me brave that Sunday morning and has given me another opportunity to speak since then.

I know where my identity and my joy comes from. It comes from **being His**.

What are you holding onto tonight that's quenching your thirst for God? Whatever it is, He already knows. **Jesus wants to help you.** He sees potential in you. You are God's child, and He hurts to see you hurting. Cling to Him tonight. **Receive joy and freedom.**

GOALS FOR THE NEW YEAR

DECEMBER 29, 2015

I'm excited to see the ways God will personally work in each of our lives this upcoming year! He is going to use us to serve Him. Here is a list of things I desire to be motivated by and accomplish each day.

- Don't surround yourself with anyone you don't wish to become like
- Even if something is not your favorite thing to do, work hard at it and succeed in becoming better to bring God glory
- Start each day off with Jesus
- Don't change yourself trying to be the person you think someone wants Be Undeniably His and remember where your identity is found
- Find joy in being different
- Be excited about life change
- Remember that Jesus wants the lost, but they have to choose Him
- Live purposefully
- Wait on God's timing and don't try to make things happen yourself
- Be pure in all that you think, say, and do
- Have a set time to pray each day, be clear of distractions, and remember all God has done
- Put your words into actions
- Be creative
- Be inspired and inspire
- Devour God's Word

- Grow in your relationship with Jesus like never before
- Be Spirit led
- Reach out, spread true joy, and show love
- Be determined and persevere
- Have accountability
- Don't underestimate what God can do
- Be the friend you wish to have
- Have fun and make memories with family
- Take advantage of the opportunities you've been given
- Remember that doing "hard" things for God will boost your growth
- Don't let people discourage you
- Be an encourager
- Grow in your spiritual gifts
- Cherish time, loved ones, opportunities, Creation, God's Word, and encounters with Jesus
- Explore and learn more about God's character
- Let your inner beauty always be the most beautiful thing about you
- Remember your commitments
- Serve God and His people

A YEAR OF MEMORIES

2016

BUT SEEK FIRST

JANUARY 3, 2016

"But seek first his kingdom and his righteousness, and all these things will be given to you as well." -Matthew 6:33 (NIV)

What is the desire of your heart today? Is it a relationship, friendship, or an answer to prayer? *Are you spending more time thinking of that one thing rather than seeking God about it?*

Having patience and exercising trust while waiting for my future husband is something I struggle with. I'm the type of person who wants to have all of the details written out, but God doesn't work that way.

Jesus knows how much we, humans, can handle. He also knows what's best and He already knows our futures. Therefore, why do we worry so much? **We shouldn't try to make things happen on our own. When we do, our plans usually leave us in worst states than what we thought we were before.**

I encourage you to keep waiting and trusting God with your desires. We have to *seek Jesus first and have Him as our top priority before we can handle the good and exciting plans He has for our lives.* Remember that God's plans are always better than our own. Let's seek Jesus with everything we have and make Him **the one true** desire of our hearts.

RESTORED BY LOVE

FEBRUARY 11, 2016

What is love? Is it holding hands, receiving gifts, taking cute pictures, or having thoughtful dates? Our society wants us to believe that love is more about words and actions rather than lifestyles. We were made with a desire for love but sometimes look to all the wrong places to find it.

I once had an unhealthy relationship in my life. I felt God telling me to let that relationship go many times, but I didn't have the strength to obey. While I was in that relationship, I was blinded to truth and became distant to those who truly knew what was best for me. I went into that relationship hoping to share Jesus' love, but my relationship with Him soon became a struggle.

Jesus is always pursuing our hearts. He hates our sins and wants us to run back to Him in order to be changed. We must turn from what's keeping us from Jesus and what's causing death in our lives. **Sometimes we don't realize why God is telling us to let go of a friendship or loved one, but we have to trust that His plans are always best.** Our Father sees the danger that lies ahead and wants to protect us from it.

When we stop worrying about earthly love in a significant other, we find the truest love in the One who loves us for eternity.

After being redeemed from that relationship in my life, I clung onto the hope of God's Word. He saw purpose and potential in me when I couldn't see it in myself. **Jesus takes us from being like the world and broken to being His**

and restored. That is love. Jesus died for us so that we could come to know Him and be changed.

I don't know where you're at today, but I want to share and speak truth to you. I want you to know that no matter how far you may feel from God, He is right there wanting you to return to Him. **Jesus' arms are open and His love for you will never end.** There's nothing that can stop God's love for you either. He sees the situation you're in and wants you to know that there's hope. He has a life full of abundance prepared for you and knows all of your desires. Matthew 6:33 tells us, *"But seek first His kingdom and His righteousness, and all these things will be given to you as well."*

In *The Chase*, Kelsey Kupecky wrote, "If we really want to put God first in our lives, we must be willing to move some things around."

Friend, I encourage you to obey the Holy Spirit today. Don't keep waiting to do what He is calling you to do. Today is the day for change and restoration. It is time to give our hearts and desires back to God!

LIVE ABUNDANTLY

FEBRUARY 22, 2016

Seasons of trial are sometimes necessary for seasons of growth.

The month of January was a hard month for me. I was struggling with things I shouldn't have been worrying about. I wondered how I was going to get through the next day and looked at the week as a giant standing before me.

"The thief cometh not, but for to steal, and to kill, and to destroy: I am come that they might have life, and that they might have it more abundantly." - John 10:10 (KJV)

There is so much hope in this verse. Jesus didn't come and die for us so that we would just "get through" each day. He came so that we could wake up joyful in His promises, know how big and mighty He is, watch Him remove our giants, free our hearts from worry and fear, live by His side, learn His character, be close to His heart, and share Him everywhere we go.

My life motto here lately has been *live abundantly.* I'm constantly reminding myself that I need to truly live and make the most of the life Jesus has given to me. The word abundance means a very large quantity of something. When you're feeling depleted of life, turn to the Giver of life. He restores our souls and gives us the strength we need for every minute of the day.

This season of trial and testing you're in isn't going to last forever. It may seem like you're stuck in the middle of darkness and chaos right now, but Jesus is offering you a way out. His timing doesn't always line up with ours, but He has a divine purpose for you being where you're at. He wants you to grow in your faith as you watch Him remove all of your fears. Know that **nothing is too big for God and nothing is impossible with Him.** Keep seeking Jesus with all of your heart, soul, mind, and strength. I promise that He will reveal Himself to you as you pursue Him.

"You will seek me and find me when you seek me with all your heart." - Jeremiah 29:13 (NIV)

Each trial that you face is another opportunity to share and show Jesus to your peers. The world is watching us. **As believers, we have something that the world doesn't, and the way we live our lives should show that.** Let's be real, loving, courageous, bold, and strong this week. *It's time for us to be the generation that steps up and leads wholeheartedly while being led by God.*

REMAIN IN HIM

FEBRUARY 29, 2016

Think of a beautiful flower. It is connected to its stem and the stem to its roots. Whenever the flower is picked, it loses connection to its nutrients and all of the things it needs to grow. In its vase, the flower will look pretty. It will only last for a short period of time. It will quickly fade away and die.

My friend, we are the flower and Jesus is our source of life. Whenever we are spending time with God in His Word and prayer, we are receiving all of the things we need to go out into the world and be different. Jesus fills us up with Himself so that we can share Him with everyone else around us daily. We grow in Him and keep coming back to Him to be satisfied. We realize that we can't live life on our own. With Jesus we can be joyful and shine radiantly.

We must remember that **without daily quiet time with God, we will soon be much farther away from Him than what we ever intended.** Whenever we neglect our walks with Jesus, we are losing the nutrients we need to live abundantly. We will grow weary and be depleted of abundant life.

"Remain in me, as I also remain in you. No branch can bear fruit by itself; it must remain in the vine. Neither can you bear fruit unless you remain in me. "I am the vine; you are the branches. If you remain in me and I in you, you will bear much fruit; apart from me you can do nothing. If you do not remain in me, you are like a branch that is thrown away and withers; such branches are picked up, thrown into the fire and burned." -John 15:4-6 (NIV)

I hope that through this post, Jesus has shown you the importance of us staying close to Him and seeking Him daily. Let's stay rooted in His love and Word and keep growing closer to Him. I challenge you to keep pursuing God even if it's hard. Know that He is and will give you the strength you need for whatever you're facing. You were made with so much purpose to change the world for His kingdom. Let's radiate Jesus' love and Presence this week. Let's display an authentic relationship with Him to the world.

A WELL-WATERED POST

MARCH 25, 2016

Just like flowers and plants, **we can't expect to be watered one time and grow fully. We have to keep being watered.**

To "keep being watered" means we have to be in continual pursuit of Christ. We should be longing for more of Jesus and filling ourselves up with Him *daily.*

On Tuesday afternoon, I was challenged to *absorb* God's Word, time with Him, and opportunities.

This school year is coming to a close, and I feel as if I need to be making the most of *every* opportunity. I don't need to look at school as wasted time. Rather, I should be striving to share God's love and light to everyone. We need to be so full of Christ that He's Who shines through our everyday lives. Our lives are not about us. As Christians, the Holy Spirit lives inside of us and **we should want to live so passionately for Him that it's contagious.**

Never forget that **there's purpose where you're placed. If we can't serve God faithfully and live for Him where we're placed now, we can't expect to serve or live for Him later.**

My challenge for us today is that we would live so closely to our Father, be watered by Him daily, and make the most of our time and opportunities. Let's shine brightly, serve Jesus well where we're placed, and treat others how He has treated us.

ETERNAL ENCOURAGEMENT & GOOD HOPE

JUNE 6, 2016

God is teaching me that His love for me doesn't depend on my behavior, how much time I spend with Him, or how much I'm serving.

"Since, then, you have been raised with Christ, set your hearts on things above, where Christ is, seated at the right hand of God. Set your minds on things above, not on earthly things. For you died, and your life is now hidden with Christ in God. When Christ, who is your life, appears, then you also will appear with him in glory." -Colossians 3:1-4 (NIV)

As believers, it's important for us to remember that God has changed us. He has given us life and a purpose. Without Christ, we are dead and live in darkness. We find life, love, joy, and peace by coming to know Jesus in a personal way.

We have the choice of what we feed. We're either going to feed our flesh or we're going to feed our spirits. Just because we're saved doesn't mean that the flesh goes away. It's something that we have to fight daily and make a decision not to feed. It can be as simple as the first thing we do in the mornings. This is something I've been convicted about lately. **It's easy to hop on social media, but I know God desires and deserves the very first part of my day.**

"May our Lord Jesus Christ himself and God our Father, who loved us and by his grace gave us eternal encouragement and good hope, encourage your hearts and strengthen you in every good deed and word." -2 Thessalonians 2:16-17 (NIV)

Because of Christ, we have **eternal encouragement and good hope**. *You have eternal encouragement and good hope. Let that encourage your heart.*

Loved one, I pray you will receive peace tonight. When you seek God, He will meet you right where you are at. Come to Him with yourself, your worries, your concerns, your fears, your mistakes, and your hurt. God is the Author and Giver of life. He is life and I pray that you experience Jesus' love to the fullest. Let's rid ourselves of the flesh daily and invest into what points us closer to Jesus.

MY YTI EXPERIENCE

JULY 10, 2016

For the past two summers, I have loved going to FUGE camp located in the mountains of North Carolina. While thinking about my summer plans for this year, I felt like God had something different for me. I just didn't know what His plans were at the time. After praying for a while, my cousin, who went to North Carolina Wesleyan College, called to tell me about a program she got an email about. I'm not the type of person who decides to do something quickly, but I had a special peace about being apart of this new program as soon as I heard about it.

It has now been a week and two days since I left North Carolina Wesleyan College. I'm excited to share my Youth Theology Institute experience with you!

The YTI was funded by a grant the college received. Its purpose is to provide rising tenth, eleventh, and twelfth grade high school students the time, place, and tools to discern God's calling upon their lives.

Each day we traveled to a place or ministry where we served, came back to campus for lunch, and had three hours of classes. We then enjoyed supper and free time along with services and small groups.

On June 26, 2016 I walked onto a college campus for the very first time and got settled into a dorm room that would be my home for a week. Sunday was a day of new beginnings and the start of new friendships. There was a total of 40 students, five counselors, three teachers, and one director. We all went on a prayer walk in nature Sunday afternoon. We occasionally stopped along the route to have object lessons.

Bright and early Monday morning, we helped with a community homeless breakfast in Rocky Mount. What stood out to me there was that the people didn't come just to be served. They felt at home, loved, and were being fed both physically and spiritually. Also, the men participated in cleaning up.

After the breakfast, we went to Peace Makers in Rocky Mount. Peace Makers is located downtown and ministers through their thrift shop, church services, Bible studies, computer lab, food drives, and summer programs for children. The staff at Peace Makers explained that they "partner" with individuals and families. **By saying partner, it's a two-way relationship. Each person has something to offer to one another.**

On Tuesday we learned how a pastor from Conetoe, North Carolina saw the needs of his community and took action in making a difference. The pastor discovered that the deaths of his friends and family members were related to genetic and health issues. The pastor now teaches valuable working skills to local young people. He also has a farm where he grows food for his community. **Our friend reminded us that our bodies are God's temples. Therefore, we should fill ourselves up with things that will be beneficial to our well-beings.** We served this ministry by cleaning their Family Life Center, staining their porch, playing with local children, and helping on the farm.

We, the YTI members, all felt an outpouring of God's presence Tuesday night. We experienced God's presence in a strong way and prayed together. It was a very special experience I will always cherish.

Wednesday morning started off with a Vocational Ministries Panel. The panel consisted of around ten adult believers from different vocations. This was one of my favorite parts of YTI. The panel talked about their backgrounds, how God changed and called them, and how they live out their faith through their vocations. Advice they could have told their younger selves was shared with us as well.

A few churches in Rocky Mount sponsored and hosted the Harlem Legends Worship Event. It was a fun time to serve the community through basketball. The Youth Theology Institute was able to help with this event by registering and greeting guests, handing out water bottles, and cleaning up after the event was over.

After a busy day, The Outpost in Rocky Mount welcomed us into their ministry for a night full of fellowship, fun, friends, team chant battles, and snacks. The Outpost offers a safe and loving environment for NCWC students. They also provide free coffee and snacks.

We went to Oakmont Baptist Church on Thursday. Located in Greenville, we learned about Oakmont's medical and housing ministry. We also had another panel.

I was talking with my counselor in her dorm room right after small group Thursday night. It was probably after 11:00, and she had to go get some campers from outside. Instead of bringing them back inside, my leader told me to come outside to watch something amazing happen. I found peers opening up, sharing their hearts, being real and honest about their struggles, and rededicating their lives to Christ! It was something amazing to be apart of and experience! Security eventually told us we had to stop and go inside because it was so late and people were trying to sleep! Camp would not have been what it was without our prayer time in the gazebo!

We had our last panel with some men from Southeastern Bible College Friday morning. After that, we packed up to go home. We ended YTI 2016 with a luncheon and a few speakers. I was honestly in tears (really trying to hold them back) as I was saying goodbyes. North Carolina Wesleyan College felt like a second home to me, and I had bonded so deeply with the people I had met.

I'm so thankful for the opportunity I had to be apart of the Youth Theology Institute. The experience, meeting brothers and sisters in Christ, forming lasting friendships, and learning more about my calling greatly impacted my life.

Although camp for this year is over, YTI is not. Each student has been placed with a mentor to grow and serve with for the next year. The Youth Theology Institute will also have a reunion in February.

A MUST READ: TIPS FOR BACK TO SCHOOL

AUGUST 4, 2016

It's crazy to think that school starts back in two weeks! I hope your summer break has been one full of making memories and the most of each day! The following pieces of advice are things I have learned or am still working on. I hope to encourage, inspire, and comfort you as you get ready for a new school year.

Audience of One

As teenagers and adults, we care a lot about what others think of us. We must be confident in who God has made us to be. We weren't made to be a clone of our best friends. *It's okay to have things in common with other people and like some of the same styles as they do, but it's never okay to buy something just to "fit in."* You were made to be unique. Stand up and be confident in who you are. *We must know who we are in Christ to know who we are fully.* It may take some courage to stand out and be different, but it's so worth it. Don't let the opinions and words of others define who you are. The only thing that should define who you are is Jesus and who you are in Him. *It's a beautiful thing when we stop being like the crowd and start being leaders for the things of Christ.*

Be Bold in and for Your Faith

Leaders lead by example. There's a special reason for you being placed where you are at. You may be one of the only believers in your class, or you may be one of many. Either way, I challenge you to be bold and courageous. Live in such a way that makes others wonder why you're so different. *We each have ways we can share the light and love of Jesus!*

If you are shy, you can write a card of encouragement, be a genuine friend, or share your own testimony.

You are not Enough on Your Own

It's important to believe in ourselves, have confidence, and do great things. Without Christ, though, we're broken, sinful, and insecure. Most importantly, we are in need of a Savior. Jesus did something for us that we could never do on our own. He died on the cross and carried the weight of our sins on His shoulders.

Image Bearers

While at camp, we talked a lot about each human bearing the image of Christ. I was convicted for judging people by their outward appearances before getting to know who they really were. Authentic and personal connections happen whenever we view people through God's lens. We should be striving to see people's hearts instead of focusing on their outward appearances.

Godly Community

I cannot over-stress the importance of keeping yourself surrounded by believers who will build you up and keep you firm when you're weak. We need people in our lives who will pray for us and with us. My church has a wonderful youth ministry that has Sunday night services. Being at church makes the biggest difference in my whole week! **Daily quiet time with God and Godly community is vital. We grow even more when those two things are combined!** We have to make sure we're being fed spiritually! Look for Godly community in your school. Having special and edifying friends with you daily will be a huge blessing!

Invest in Growth

While being in school, there are many of opportunities to find what you're passionate about. I started Yearbook last fall. Because of being on the team, I've grown and gotten so much better in photography. I challenge you to take advantage of the opportunities you have been given. Try a few different things or just grow in what you already love to do. Having a fun elective will help you truly enjoy school!

Don't neglect your relationships as you invest into your passions and talents. Most importantly, strive to keep growing closer to God!

What Lasts for Eternity

Due to being so stressed out in eighth grade, I cried myself to sleep a few times. Since then, I've learned that while school and grades are important, we shouldn't let them ruin our lives! **Stress never makes things better.** When we are actually enjoying school, managing our time well, and doing what we're supposed to do, things will hopefully go much better. **Don't get so caught up in the now that you completely forget about long-term**. Let's invest into what's important.

Stay Connected to Your Power Source

Without your Source, you will fall. I want to see each of us stay strong even through storms this upcoming year. In order to stay strong, we have to stay connected to our Source of life, love, joy, and hope! We have to make praying and reading God's Word a daily priority in our lives. It's amazing to see God reveal Himself to us as we clear our lives of distractions.

Your Journey

Don't be ashamed of your past any longer. Your mistakes do not define you. God used your struggles to make you into who you are today. We can't change what's already happened, but we can learn from our past experiences. We can readily help others who are struggling with the same things we once faced. No matter how your life used to be, start focusing on who you are today. God has BIG things prepared for you. Let Him take you as you are and make you new. He will restore you and make you whole. God has loved you for all of time. His love for you never ends.

Victory Days

This past year, I was really struggling with fear and anxiety. It was a hard battle, but I learned to claim victory over it each day of my life! I challenge you to wake up each morning and remind yourself that *today is a victory day*. **You have already won the battle because of your Dad being Jesus.** He is always fighting for us, and the enemy has no power over us. Whenever you start to feel weak, remember that *today is a victory day.*

Here's to another school year!

BEING> DOING

AUGUST 24, 2016

Last school year, I baked for my class with the purpose of sharing God's love. I also wrote cards to show my peers that I cared about them. I did these things with right and pure motives.

When things start to become familiar, though, it's easy to do them out of habit. If we're not careful, our actions will be led by what we want others to think of us. We will do Godly acts of kindness and participate in Christian clubs and events. We must ask ourselves why we are doing the things we are participating in. We should do all things to glorify God and point others to Him.

I have recently been worried that if I am not baking, writing, or constantly giving encouragement that my fruit isn't going to be evident. I have also wondered if my light is shining as it should be.

Someone at the United Conference said, "Jesus is more concerned with you *being* rather than *doing*."

We're always busy on the go. We falsely believe that the things we're doing define who we are. Jesus wants us to be focused on Him. When we're focused on Him, we are growing, being molded, and will have the fruit of God's Spirit evident in our lives. Jesus' characteristics will be what comes out of us whenever we fill ourselves up with Him. Our flesh and spirits are in constant war.

Listed below are a few plans of action to take in having victory over the flesh:

- Have meaningful time in the Bible and prayer **daily**

- Invest in the friendships and things that point you closer to Christ. These friendships and things will set your soul more on fire for Him.
- Realize your weaknesses and pray about them
- Focus on your beauty that comes from within
- Be so focused on Jesus, who He is, and your relationship with Him
- Live for an audience of One
- Make sure you're being spiritually fed and filled
- Live out your faith

Let yourself rest in Jesus tonight, tomorrow, and every day. Find your peace and joy in being with God, and watch the ways He will do amazing things through you. Your fruit is evident. Your light is shining.

THE THINGS UNSEEN

SEPTEMBER 25, 2016

The purpose of this life is more about the things unseen.

A few minutes ago while praying, I found myself tired and worn out from worrying so much about temporary things. I've been trying to keep our house spotless, the TV controls in their designated spot, and all of the laundry folded a particular way.

Jesus reminded me that as much as a house is cleaned, it's never going to be perfect. It's constantly going to keep getting dirty and need to be repaired. A house is to be lived in. It is a place where you dwell with those you love most. Although homes do have to be taken care of, we must not obsess over them.

You and I are much like treasured homes. We're God's holy temples. We seek to live for Jesus but fall into sin daily. God is always there for us, investing into us, and making us better. **We will never be perfect, but we have a Father who is invested into making us most like Himself.**

Obsessing and busying ourselves with temporary things will only make us worn out and exhausted.

While in the mountains this past week, I watched a potter take a blob of clay, and make it into something beautiful. The pottery didn't become beautiful on its own. All it did was exist and be in the hands of the potter. We are the clay that's nothing but ugly until Jesus starts to reshape and purify us.

"Yet you, Lord, are our Father. We are the clay, you are the potter; we are all the work of your hand." -Isaiah 64:8 (NIV)

Seasons of the year, seasons of friendships, seasons of relationships, and seasons of passions are constantly changing.

God allowed me to be apart of someone's life last year. He also used that person to influence my life. I was able to encourage and be there for my friend; while he helped me to enjoy the day, not be so serious, and think about things differently. As the school year ended and changes were made in our lives, I realized that our season of friendship was coming to a close.

I learned that God has a plan for us being exactly in the school, classroom, seating arrangement, family, or job we're in. These things are not by mistake. As I look back on the season I had with my friend, I now wish I had started to invest into him way before I did. **Don't wait on anything to start making a difference today.** *Just because a school year or job ends on a certain day, doesn't mean that you have that much time to spend with someone.* We're not guaranteed tomorrow.

Also, if you're having a hard time letting go of someone, remember that *you should never stop praying for them.* Our prayers can do more than what we ever could do on our own.

Pastor Anthony Braswell, who spoke at the United Conference, stated, *"Sermons and songs aren't going to change the world. Rather, it's the love of Jesus shining in your life."*

As we head into a new week, remember that you're so loved and important. The sacrifices you make and the hard work you do doesn't go unnoticed. It's making a difference. Let yourself rest. Stop and breathe. Invest into the people God has placed in your life. Let His light shine through you each day.

NOTES TO SELF:

OCTOBER 3, 2016

In the busy world we live in, it is sometimes difficult to stop, rest, and be reminded of what's important in life. The words I'm sharing with you are from a journal entry I wrote to myself. My desire is that this simple post would encourage, motivate, and challenge you.

- Life is only meaningful when lived for and with Jesus
- Make the most of the opportunities you've been given
- Explore ministry to determine your calling
- Don't worry. Instead, cast all of your cares on the Lord. He has already carried them so you wouldn't have to
- Pray for others more
- Cling to the Rock and continue to build yourself upon Him.
- Only surround yourself with people you wish to become like. Choose friends who point you closer to Jesus
- Go to Sunday night services
- Mature in every way
- Keep God first
- Continue to grow in your gifts
- Encourage, uplift, and inspire
- Be a friend
- Don't stress
- Live abundantly

- Make the most of every breath you are given
- Look forward to things but live intentionally daily
- Be watchful for the needs of others
- Clear yourself of distractions
- Tune into the voice of God
- Remember that your relationship with God is the most important relationship you'll ever have
- Invest into those around you
- Help others find who they are in Christ

YOUR INHERITANCE

OCTOBER 20, 2016

"See that no one is sexually immoral, or is godless like Esau, who for a single meal sold his inheritance rights as the oldest son. Afterward, as you know, when he wanted to inherit this blessing, he was rejected. Even though he sought the blessing with tears, he could not change what he had done." -Hebrews 12:16-17 (NIV)

Imagine that someone in your family spent their whole life working towards something. They lost sleep over it, invested time and money into it, and gave it their all. It was their life. As your loved one got older and then passed away, everything they had worked hard for became yours. You weren't the one who had invested your life into the business, job, or ministry. Although you hadn't lost a wink of sleep over it or given a penny to fund it, your inheritance changed your life for the better.

In Genesis 25:19-24, one brother exchanged his birthright for a bowl of stew. Because the birthright was given to Esau, the oldest child, he would receive everything his father owned whenever his father passed away. Being hungry and famished, Esau went into his family's house. His brother, Jacob, had some stew. Esau didn't care what he had to do to fill his hunger. He, therefore, ended up giving his birthright to Jacob.

He sold his inheritance for a single meal.

Hebrews 12:16-17 tells us that Esau could not change what he had done. Although he realized his mistake and begged to get the birthright back with tears, Esau's mistake was final.

You, my special friend, have an inheritance that you may or may not know about. You have a loved One Whose purpose was to give this inheritance to you. Jesus did not just invest His life into it but He gave His life. You could not and cannot do anything to earn this inheritance. You couldn't work hard enough or be good enough for it either. All you can do is accept the best gift of eternal life. It is an inheritance that lasts for eternity.

If you realize this gift that you have been offered, have you accepted it?

Have you been selling or trading your inheritance in for a one time pleasure?

My desire and burden is that you would not throw away your eternal inheritance. Please do not trade it in for something that will fade away. If you still have breath in your lungs, it's not too late to claim and take your gift back. Salvation and redemption is always available to you because God's love for you isn't based off of who you are, what you have, or what you can do. God doesn't need you, but He wants you.

Do not wait until you meet Jesus face to face to desire your gift of eternal life with Him. At that point, it is too late. Your time is right now to get right with Him.

"Then the King will say to those on his right, 'Come, you who are blessed by my Father; take your inheritance, the kingdom prepared for you since the creation of the world." -Matthew 25:34 (NIV)

"Then shall he say also unto them on the left hand, Depart from me, ye cursed, into everlasting fire, prepared for the devil and his angels:" -Matthew 25:41 (KJV)

"And these shall go away into everlasting punishment: but the righteous into life eternal." -Matthew 25:46 (KJV)

TRIALS AND TESTING

OCTOBER 29, 2016

On Instagram, I recently shared some thoughts on what my friends and I were struggling with. I typed, "Are having a bad week or facing opposition from many directions? I've got some good news for you. Joy, freedom, life change, and world shaking is on the verge of happening. **The reason the enemy works against us is because of the power of Jesus working within us!** If we weren't a threat to the enemy, we wouldn't be a target to tear down. Know what's happening and stay strong. What we're living for lasts forever. The narrow path may not always be easy, but it's always worth it. Keep confusing people by giving and showing love when they persecute, upset, or make fun of you. I'm cheering for you."

I want to share some verses with you that the Lord has used to encourage my heart this week.

"It is for freedom that Christ has set us free. Stand firm, then, and do not let yourselves be burdened again by a yoke of slavery." -Galations 5:1 (NIV)

"Consider it pure joy, my brothers and sisters, whenever you face trials of many kinds, because you know that the testing of your faith produces perseverance. Let perseverance finish its work so that you may be mature and complete, not lacking anything." -James 1:2-4 (NIV)

"Blessed is the one who perseveres under trial because, having stood the test, that person will receive the crown of life that the Lord has promised to those who love him." -James 1:12 (NIV)

"But whoever looks intently into the perfect law that gives freedom, and continues in it—not forgetting what they have heard, but doing it—they will be blessed in what they do." -James 1:25 (NIV)

"Finally, all of you, be like-minded, be sympathetic, love one another, be compassionate and humble. Do not repay evil with evil or insult with insult. On the contrary, repay evil with blessing, because to this you were called so that you may inherit a blessing." -1 Peter 3:8-9 (NIV)

"The end of all things is near. Therefore be alert and of sober mind so that you may pray. Above all, love each other deeply, because love covers over a multitude of sins. Offer hospitality to one another without grumbling. Each of you should use whatever gift you have received to serve others, as faithful stewards of God's grace in its various forms. If anyone speaks, they should do so as one who speaks the very words of God. If anyone serves, they should do so with the strength God provides, so that in all things God may be praised through Jesus Christ. To him be the glory and the power for ever and ever. Amen." -1 Peter 4:7-11 (NIV)

"In the same way, the Spirit helps us in our weakness. We do not know what we ought to pray for, but the Spirit himself intercedes for us through wordless groans. And he who searches our hearts knows the mind of the Spirit, because the Spirit intercedes for God's people in accordance with the will of

God. And we know that in all things God works for the good of those who love him, who have been called according to his purpose." -Romans 8:26-28 (NIV)

"No, in all these things we are more than conquerors through him who loved us." -Romans 8:37 (NIV)

GOD HAS ALREADY WON

NOVEMBER 7, 2016

Reading through my old journals, an entry from June 2, 2015 stood out to me. I knew I had to share it with you as a lot of focus has been on our country and election lately.

"I know it's not good to worry about the future, but my mind has been thinking a lot today. Will our next president be a man of God? Are we close to the end times? Will our nation turn back to God? Throughout history, bad things have happened, people thought they were living in the last days, and there has been some major turning to and from Jesus. All we can do is pray, stand up for what's right, and put action behind our faith. Sometimes God allows bad things to happen so that we will see we are nothing without Him. Jesus is our only hope. This world isn't our home. We are here with purpose to proclaim and share Jesus Christ. We don't have to move across the world to share the love and Gospel of Jesus. It starts in our homes, neighborhoods, schools, and cities. People all around us are slaves to sin and in need of chains being broken. We can offer them true freedom through the blood of Jesus. Our country and world still has hope because the love of Jesus is still radiating and changing the hearts of His people. The devil may be getting a few smiles, but **God has already won.**"

NEVER TIRE

NOVEMBER 13, 2016

We can't worry about tomorrow if we are only focusing on today.

This past week has been one of living in true freedom. Last Sunday night, my youth pastor reminded me to not worry. God will take care of our every need considering He does so for birds and flowers.

"Look at the birds of the air; they do not sow or reap or store away in barns, and yet your heavenly Father feeds them. Are you not much more valuable than they?" -Matthew 6:26 (NIV)

"If that is how God clothes the grass of the field, which is here today and tomorrow is thrown into the fire, will he not much more clothe you—you of little faith?" -Matthew 6:30 (NIV)

Walking out of the house Monday morning, the first thing I saw was a little bird on the patio. It was a sweet reminder of what Jesus taught me the night before. Most of the things I usually worry about are small and probably won't ever happen. Learning how to just trust Jesus with my thoughts and knowing He will provide for my every need is such a comfort.

We should serve God through every opportunity despite how small it may seem.

God has provided opportunities for me to extend His love this week. Some of those opportunities included praying for someone, writing cards of encouragement, comforting a person who was upset, or walking beside someone who didn't want to face a battle alone. Jesus has placed us right where we're at to serve and build His kingdom. **It's not about who is doing the work of God. Rather, it's about Who the work of God is being done for.** *We sometimes have to remind ourselves that this life isn't about us.*

"And as for you, brothers and sisters, never tire of doing what is good." -2 Thessalonians 3:13 (NIV)

Never tire of doing what is good. Your life may be busy, and I know you have a lot going on, but keep doing good and seeking Jesus first. He is with you, hears you, cares for you, and will provide for your every need. I pray that you believe these things, and learn how to live in true freedom this week. You are a difference maker.

WHERE YOUR HEART IS

DECEMBER 19, 2016

"For where your treasure is, there your heart will be also." -Matthew 6:21 (NIV)

In the midst of reading passages that I wasn't really comprehending, this verse stood out to me. I decided to stop and really think about it.

What am I holding onto with a tight grasp? *Social media. Running myself crazy trying to do so much that's not really necessary.*

Where do I *want* my heart to be? *Close to my Father's heart, in His will, and doing His kingdom work through ministry.*

To think and live as Christ is to forsake what comes naturally. It's so easy to get upset, blame others, and try to find our purpose in our work when we're living in the flesh.

We have life in, because, and through Jesus. The purpose of our lives on earth is to know God, love Him, live in Him, and share Him. Jesus is our purpose. Once we realize that our purpose is rooted in a mission bigger than ourselves, we can't live selfish lives. It will no longer be about what we can do, but what God can do through us. Without Christ, we are broken, helpless, and pitiful humans living temporary lives. *With Christ, we are made whole, hopeful, and living with the promise of eternal life in Heaven.*

"For our struggle is not against flesh and blood, but against the rulers, against the authorities, against the powers of this dark world and against the spiritual forces of evil in the heavenly realms." -Ephesians 6:12 (NIV)

"The world and its desires pass away, but whoever does the will of God lives forever." -1 John 2:17 (NIV)

What are you going to do to refocus your perspective, live for a bigger purpose, and grasp what's really important?

Let's take the time to answer this question. I'll share my answers with you hoping you will be challenged and encouraged by them.

- fast
- be instead of do
- have accountability
- pray and be **devoted** to being in God's Word <u>daily</u>
- make time for the things that are most important
- limit time on social media
- dream big-believe even bigger-pray for the best
- go out of my comfort zone to do God's will
- be humble and full of Christ
- surround myself with the believers God has placed in my life

I am so thankful for you and your life. We're in this journey together, and I'm here to keep cheering you on even when you feel like giving up. God has so much in store for your life. I pray that you find rest and peace in Him tonight. Amazing things happen when we stop, sit, and let Him do what only He can do.

10 THINGS I LEARNED IN 2016

DECEMBER 29, 2016

---

1. Love is not based off of behavior

Mr. Wright, my former Bible teacher, shared this quote in class. It stayed in my mind and challenged my heart. Despite a person's mood, we are called to love them in a way that reflects our Father's love for us. Also, it is a great comfort knowing that God's love for us isn't based off of our good works or time spent with Him. Jesus' love is given to us because of His sacrifice on the cross.

2. How to live abundantly

Seasons of trial are sometimes necessary for seasons of growth.

3. What it means to be free indeed

When Jesus sets us free from our past sins and struggles, those things are washed away. They no longer define who we are. We are new creations. John 8:36 (NIV) says, **"So if the Son sets you free, you will be free indeed."**

4. Grow in my gifts

Last Christmas, I received my own camera. Since then, I've experienced so much joy while capturing moments that only happen once. I've also been able to use my love for photography in ministry, and that makes me even happier.

Each Sunday morning, I spend time with the sweetest preschoolers. They teach me so much about life through their perspective of things. Seeing the little kids love Jesus at such a young age reminds me of my life's purpose.

5. The plans of God are revealed in the Presence of God

    Jesus has shown me that He directs us through His peace and Presence.

6. Nothing can stop or stand in the way of the plans God has for your life

7. My passion for ministry

    While leading Impact Bible Study and helping with the MORE group at school, I had so many opportunities to reach others. I was able to encourage, equip, and be an example to those around me. Our group was humbled to find out someone received salvation in a chapel service we helped planned.

8. The importance of Godly community and deep friendships

    We were never created to do life alone. *We feel most alive whenever we are in God's will surrounded by those He has given to us to do life with.* Jesus has allowed me to get connected in my youth group and make deep connections with friends who also have a purpose and passion for the things of God. Whenever we are surrounding ourselves with Godly people and building deep friendships with them, there will be joy bursting out of our souls.

9. The meaning behind victory days

    The purpose of victory days isn't to be confident in our own strength. *Victory days remind us in our weakest moments that God's strength and peace is always more than enough for us. They challenge us to persevere, walk boldly, and live abundantly whenever we're tempted to stop, hide, and fear.*

10. Treasure family, friends, moments, and memories

This year has been good. It started out full of trials but has ended as a season of growth. Jesus has become the one true desire of my heart and has taught me so many lessons through our walks and talks together. He has filled my days with family, friends, moments, and memories I will hold close to my heart forever.

A YEAR OF LIFE

2017

I AM A CHILD OF GOD

JANUARY 3, 2017

Hey, sweet friend. The start to this week and new year has already been full of messy life and challenging moments. It has also been filled with freedom, peace, and a call to live fully *now*.

Life is not about the amount of time we will have but what we do with the amount of time we've been given.

My heart is burdened for lost, broken, hurt, and wandering people. I'm being challenged to live with everything I have in order to bring about change, hope, and true life to those around me.

What are we doing to make an impact on this world for Jesus today? Jesus loves you more than any human heart ever could. Have you accepted Him? Are you giving Him your very best?

Jesus died to save *everyone*. **No matter how bad you think your sin is, it isn't beyond forgiveness.** Jesus, being perfect, took all of your sins, pains, struggles, and heart aches so that you would be freed from them.

This is a new year. Each breath you breathe brings another opportunity to be made new. Jesus is the only true Hope we have. I beg you to stop putting your trust in temporary people and things.

You have an opportunity in this moment to be made new.

My soul's desire tonight is that we would stop hiding behind our failures, pasts, and fears. We must live these lives we've been given with every fiber of our beings. Let's bring Life, Hope, and Healing to a dead, broken, and hurt land.

The following words have been ministering to my heart here lately. I hope they become the song of your heart as well.

I am a Child of God

I am no longer a slave to fear. The old is gone, and the new is here.

I am a child of God!

I am being transformed by the renewing of my mind as I leave the sins and struggles of my past behind.

I am a child of God!

I will walk about in perfect peace knowing my joy will increase.

I am a child of God!

MORE IN STORE

JANUARY 14, 2017

What wounds are you hiding?

God desires to use the nasty, embarrassing, and hurtful wounds we hide to tell beautiful stories of hope and redemption.

In his book *It's Not What You Think*, Jefferson Bethke wrote, "Only when a wound is a scar will we let it tell a story." God is the only One Who can heal our hearts and wounds. Psalm 147:3 (NIV) states, "He heals the brokenhearted and binds up their wounds."

God has *more in store* for the embarrassing, ugly, and hurtful sins of our pasts along with the mistakes of our present. Once we ask for forgiveness, Jesus doesn't hold our past sins or mistakes against us. **He doesn't want us to live feeling guilty. Rather, He wants us to live free.**

"You intended to harm me, but God intended it for good to accomplish what is now being done, the saving of many lives." -Genesis 50:20 (NIV)

Hard times and hurtful experiences are not to harm us. Instead, they provide opportunities for us to grow closer to God, rely on His strength, and encourage others who will face the same struggles we have experienced.

We hide wounds but are proud to tell others the stories behind our scars. *Scars show that although we've experienced pain, we've been healed.* **Scars provide opportunities to share what God has done in us and for us.**

God's love for you isn't based off of your behavior or anything you could ever do on your own. His love is given freely by grace, and nothing can separate you from it.

I challenge you to stop hiding your wounds, allow Jesus to be your Healer, and share God's goodness through your scars.

BE ROOTED

FEBRUARY 5, 2017

Your light in the darkness shines so bright. Because you stand out, you are a larger target to aim at.

The enemy is reminded of his own destiny whenever you choose to fight and continue to seek God. He is also reminded that *every* knee **will** bow, and *every* tongue **will** confess that Jesus Christ is Lord (Philippians 2:10-11).

You are a threat to the enemy. You have Power living within you that he can never touch. You are the bright light in the darkness. You are victorious. It doesn't matter how much discouragement you face because you are a child of God. The Creator of Heaven and Earth is on your side. Nothing formed against God shall stand, and if He is for you, then who can be against you (Romans 8:31)?

Your thoughts of doubt shall be no more. Our God is real, and He is on the move. Our God is with us. He will never leave us nor forsake us (Deuteronomy 31:6).

You have a special gift, Power, and Light within you that needs to be spread. It can't be put out.

God has a plan bigger than we can see to use our gifts and lives to build His kingdom in a powerful way. We must keep our hearts, minds, eyes, and lives *rooted* in Jesus. When winds of the world come against us, we can stand firm and not be shaken. We will continue to flourish, and be who God has created us to be.

EYES ON HIM

FEBRUARY 7, 2017

I never want to fall away from Jesus. Thinking of falling into temptation, the current of likeness, and the stream of this world ignites fear within me.

Being Undeniably His means to stand out, shine bright, and let our love for God be where our identity is found. It also means living for a purpose bigger than ourselves. Having a personal relationship with Jesus allows you and I to see life through a new lens. *It brings life's purpose from black and white into vivid color.* We no longer work for human satisfaction or worldly gains. Having our eyes on Jesus automatically assures us that:

1. We aren't walking alone
2. We aren't accomplishing things by our own strength
3. Impossible things are made more than possible through Jesus Christ

We do not and cannot worry about falling away from Jesus and into the streams of this world whenever our eyes are on our Father. As our eyes are on Jesus, He is leading and guiding us. We aren't walking into things on our own.

Jesus called Peter, one of His disciples, to walk on water towards Him. With human strength, that was impossible. It definitely wasn't an everyday request.

Join me as we look at Matthew 14:22-32 (NIV), and apply it to our own lives.

Matthew 14:22-32

v. 25,26- Jesus was walking on the water towards His disciples. Because the disciples saw something happen bigger than themselves, they became afraid.

v. 27- "But Jesus immediately said to them: 'Take courage! It is I. Don't be afraid.'"

v. 28- Peter wanted confirmation that it was God (and not a ghost) walking towards them on the water.

v. 29- Jesus told Peter to "come". Then Peter got out of the boat, walked on the water, and went towards Jesus.

Amazing and miraculous things happen when we choose to take our eyes off of ourselves and our doubts. We must fix our eyes on Jesus, where He's at, and where He is leading us to go.

v. 30- After Peter obeyed, trusted Jesus, and started on a unique journey, he was faced with opposition and became afraid.

When the winds of life come our way, we can't take our eyes off of the One Who is holding us up. We have to hold onto Him even more.

Also, when we are doing miraculous things by God's power, we can't become confident in ourselves. That is when we will fall.

v. 31- "Immediately Jesus reached out his hand and caught him. 'You of little faith,' he said, 'why did you doubt?'"

Trials and temptations will come our way, but we can rest in the fact that Jesus will always give us strength and victory.

What are you struggling with tonight, friend? I am here to encourage you to keep walking towards Jesus. Please continue to keep your eyes focused on Him. God is holding your hand, leading you, and calling out to you. Don't allow the winds around you to keep you from seeing all that He has in store for you. You are a world changer. I am so thankful for the opportunity to live for a Purpose bigger than myself. I hope you are too. We don't deserve anything good. Yet, God continues to fill our lives with not only good but Godly things. He is always for us, hearing us, and fighting for us.

    Praying for your heart,
    Haley

16 YEARS OF LIFE

FEBRUARY 9, 2017

As a child, my friends and I dreamed of the days we would eventually turn sixteen and get our licenses. We said that we would go shopping and have a ton of beach trips in the summer.

Today is the day I embrace being sixteen. My journey of life so far has been full of family, friends, magical summers, heartfelt winters, lessons being learned, adventures, school, and my love for God increasing.

A few of my favorite childhood memories include playing with baby dolls, dressing up in my mom's clothes, hating sleep, and absolutely being obsessed with dogs (I always wanted a yellow lab).

I've seen my family receive things we once prayed for.

I've realized that it takes being "broken" of our flesh and human craving of love to be made whole and live in the love God has already given to us.

I've learned that God uses each and every part of our stories to make us exactly into who He has created us to be.

I want to share 16 things with you that I have learned. These are things I would tell my past or future self.

1. God is the only One who will never change.
2. Recognize beauty in all the places it shines and hides.
3. Life is so short. Therefore, make the most of every opportunity you get.
4. You will never regret being set apart. It will not always be easy, but you would much rather stand out than fit in.

5. Respect your parents, what they say, and their advice over your life.
6. Fashion and outward beauty will fade away. Don't allow your identity to be found in anyone or anything other than belonging to Jesus and being His child.
7. Guard your heart. Trust God to bring your earthly love into your life in His timing. Don't try to make things happen on your own.
8. Your relationship with Jesus is the most important relationship you'll ever have. Treasure it and invest into it daily.
9. Overflow with thankfulness for all God has done and blessed you with.
10. Be an overachiever and always do more than what's expected.
11. View others as image bearers of God.
12. What you fill yourself up with will be what you overflow with.
13. Comparison only makes you forget how blessed you are and the unique story God has given you.
14. God wants those who are lost and has already paid the price for them to have eternal life with Him.
15. God has purpose in every season you will ever live in.
16. Find your gifts and grow in them. Use the things you are passionate about to serve and build God's kingdom.

I am praying that the 16 things I shared with you will speak to you, encourage you, and remind you to live this life with all you have. Let's make a difference for eternity today!

Your friend,

Haley

DURING THE JOURNEY

MARCH 3, 2017

Life is moving along so quickly! It is sometimes hard to stop on the sidelines to see how far we've come because we are constantly running towards what's ahead. Although our eyes have to be focused on the finish line and the Prize, there are a few helpful tips to remember during the journey.

1. You have to rest and stay hydrated in order to persevere.

I realize how crazy busy our schedules are, but rest is vital for our health both physically and spiritually. Without daily walks and talks with the Lord, it is so easy for me to be irritable, unpleasant, and without joy. We can't neglect our spiritual needs.

2. Don't compare your timeline to those behind, beside, or ahead of you.

One of my favorite quotes is "Comparison is the thief of joy" by Theodore Roosevelt. Jesus has each of us in different seasons for a reason. *When we desire to be where others are at, we forget the importance of where God has us now. Instead of being jealous of people who are experiencing things we haven't, we should be joyful for them.* Although that is challenging, it is important. If our eyes are only focused on what's behind or ahead of us, we will miss out on what God has in front of us.

3. Encourage those running beside you.

In PE, there would always be girls running at different paces. The fast runners would be beside each other, and the slow runners (like myself) would rely on each other's company, encouragement, and laughs to endure each mile. We shouldn't compare ourselves to others, but we should have friends to work towards the finish line with. Having friends who share the same beliefs as we do makes the journey of life exciting. We should have friends who we can encourage, pray for, and cheer on.

4. Celebrate every victory!

After attempting to get contacts for two years, I finally got them this week! It reminded me to stop and celebrate every victory no matter how small one may seem. What have you been working towards? *Life is too short to be stingy with celebration.*

TO THE ONE WHO QUESTIONS THEIR GIFTS

MARCH 31, 2017

Your calling is not guaranteed to be easy or done without effort.

If you are like me, you have probably desired to quit something before because you believed lies of the enemy, felt insecure, and saw others doing it better.

I recently realized that my calling didn't have to be done without effort to be meaningful.

I remember sitting at the piano for hours as a young child. As soon as I met the age requirement at my school, I started taking lessons. Practicing every day was a pain and I did not enjoy meeting my weekly practice goals. In middle school, I was embarrassed to play in front of my classmates who were more experienced in piano than I was. Playing piano has never been what I first tell people about myself. Despite my deep desire to quit taking piano lessons, there was always something deep within me pulling against that hard decision. I continued to take lessons as I entered high school with a new teacher.

God has been teaching me that when we are able to accomplish something completely on our own, His strength is limited in the places it can shine.

I believe that God designed each one of us intricately. *We are made up of many tiny details, and He knows each one.* When did we start believing that we could only be used by God in the things we do gracefully are proud of? My Father has convicted me to not limit the ways He can use me.

God has more opportunities to show Himself through us whenever we cannot accomplish something on our own. What opportunities has He given you?

We are all instruments God desires to use to be a part of the most beautiful song.

CRIES IN THE DESERT

APRIL 10, 2017

Jesus saved the Israelites from their enemies at the Red Sea to make His power known. The Israelites believed God's promises and sang praises to Him after their enemies were killed. Psalm 106:13-14 (NIV) says, "But they soon forgot what he had done and did not wait for his plan to unfold. In the desert they gave in to their craving; in the wilderness they put God to the test." Psalm 106:43-44 (NIV) tells us, "Many times he delivered them, but they were bent on rebellion and they wasted away in their sin. Yet he took note of their distress when he heard their cry."

We readily praise God after He redeems us from a bad situation or answers a prayer we've been praying for years. Months after the miraculous things happen, though, do we forget the good things God did for us? Are we trying to make things happen on our own rather than waiting for His plan to unfold?

The desert is a dry place where fruit and beauty barely exists. There is a longing for water in a desert.

When we are in a desert, do we give in to our cravings? Like the Israelites, we have all wandered away from God's truth, forgot His goodness, and got tired of waiting for His plan to unfold.

When God parted the Red Sea, He knew each path the Israelites would take after that day. As the people praised Him, God knew they would quickly forget what He had done for them.

God knew in advance the hurt and rejection people would cause Him, but that didn't change the way He treated or loved them.

Our Father is more patient, forgiving, and caring than any of us ever could be. No matter how far away we may feel from God, He hears us when we cry out to Him.

JUST STOP

MAY 15, 2017

Stop. Lift your eyes from your phone, sit down, take a walk, and seek sweet conversation with the Lord. You probably don't hear these words often. Your kids are hungry. Your house (and car) needs to be cleaned. You're trying to juggle the responsibilities that come along with the many different roles you fulfill. You wonder if your spouse or roommate notices the things you do for them. When people ask how you're doing, you often respond by saying *"busy"*.

    As you live through your daily routine, there's a Power Source within you that's waiting to be tapped into. You may be *feeling* distant from the Lord today, but I beg you to remember Truth. Your Heavenly Father loves you just as much today as He did the day you first became His child. God has never stopped watching over you. As you sleep, He makes sure you are safe and provided for. *You have never taken a step where Jesus hasn't already walked.* He goes before you. Psalm 139:5 (NIV) says, "You hem me in behind and before, and you lay your hand upon me."

    God's creation is praising Him and bringing Him glory by *being.* There are so many lessons we can learn from our Father's masterpieces. Have you forgotten that you are hand crafted and a unique piece of art as well? Your life was not a mistake. The Lord knew you before you existed. Your eyes sparkle with His love, and you are filled with gifts that belong to God. You have an incredible opportunity and responsibility to use your gifts to build His kingdom. By yourself, you can't do everything. But with Christ, you are strong. He alone is always more than enough. Do you remember the days you wept and prayed for the things you have now? Your Dad saw and knew each and every detail of your heart. He saved His best for you, and has given you patience to not settle for less.

I know this life feels like it is spinning and never stops, but the Lord calls us to stop in the midst of it all to seek His face. **In a million years from now, the only thing that will matter is the time you've spent with Jesus, how you've served Him, and how used your time to invest into others.**

No one has a perfect or polished life. Stop being so hard on yourself. Don't compare yourself to anyone else. Be Undeniably His. As Jesus whispers to you, I challenge you to quiet the noises around you so that you can hear His voice and rest in His Presence. You'll never be in a place where Jesus doesn't want you or love you. His heart is full of redemption. He writes the most beautiful stories. Don't give up on your relationship with God or the ministries He has placed within you.

My prayer is that we keep chasing after Jesus even when our sides hurt and we're out of breath.

GIVING OUR BEST

MAY 22, 2017

God uses and multiplies what we give Him in much bigger ways than we could ever dream of.

    The ride home from school was unlike usual. I was tired, ill, hungry, and not in a good mood. There are only a few days left of the school year, and I need to study for exams. In order to receive some peace, I put my sunglasses and tennis shoes on and started walking. I'm sure you're also a little worn out from your busy schedule!

    In Luke 9, we are challenged to *view problems through God's power rather than viewing them through human perspectives.* I pray the following truths I share with you will encourage you, motivate you, challenge you, and help you finish the year strong.

1. We, as God's children, have the Power *living within* us that heals the sick, raises the dead to life, and drives out demons. Our Father has already overcome the whole world!

2. Before Jesus fed over 5,000 people, He knew what His Father was capable of doing. *When Jesus solved problems through His Father's power, people were amazed and needs were more than met.*

3. **Jesus always does more than what's expected.** He took a meal that would normally feed one person and used it to feed over 5,000 people! Jesus could

have sent the men and their families away hungry to find food for themselves, but He wanted to personally meet their needs.

4. We may not think we have much to offer, but God can use and multiply our offerings in bigger ways than we could imagine. Have you ever thought about the little boy who gave Jesus the fish and loaves of bread? That little boy could have been selfish, but he wasn't. **The boy invested what he had into what he could not see because he trusted in the One Whose power is unlimited.** The story in Luke 9 shows that the boy had faith in what God could do.

What you have to offer is important to God and can change the lives of those around you! Never forget the importance of your life, gifts, talents, or time. God has bigger things in store for you than what you can even imagine. Hand him your best and trust Him with the rest. God is always for you and fighting for you! He loves you!

Let's remember these truths as we finish out the year strong!

Here for you,

Haley

BUGS & NUDGES

MAY 30, 2017

"God knew the desire of your heart" is the phrase of words my mom said as we walked out of the Aldi store. I was filled with thankfulness as I looked at my tiny car. God began to stir something within me. **He places nudges and thoughts within us that should not be ignored.**

I honestly hadn't been praying about what car I would get. Before I had my permit, I didn't even have an interest in cars. As a child, I did love Volkswagen Beetles. During the car searching process, I started looking at other brands. I thought I wanted something bigger. Meanwhile, my dad kept asking me about Volkswagen bugs. *I knew something was special about them, but I didn't fully know why. I now look back and see that God gave me hints to what His plan was.*

One of the ways God gives us hints to His future plans for us is through nudges. The definition of nudge is to push against gently, especially in order to gain attention or give a signal. Another definition is to urge into action.

As a child, all I knew was that for some reason, I was drawn to Volkswagen Beetles. I had no clue that my Heavenly Father had a detailed plan to bless me with one. Before I was born, my dad met a man that was his principal and co-worker. My dad lost his dear friend a year before I turned sixteen. My dad found out that his friend's car was going to be sold. It happened to be a 2013 black Volkswagen Beetle.

Do you see God's fingerprints?

The purpose of sharing this story is to remind you of a few things.

1. Jesus knows the deepest desires of your heart
2. Jesus cares and acts upon the desires of your heart
3. Jesus gives us clues to pay attention to in order to follow and discern what His will is

Based off of God's goodness to me in this story, I can't even imagine what He has planned for the things I have prayed about. Our God is faithful and gracious in the small and big things.

CHOOSING WHAT IS BETTER

JUNE 11, 2017

Choosing what is better requires sacrifice, dedication, and discipline.

In Luke 10:38-42, a woman named Martha prepared her home to welcome Jesus into it. I can imagine she was cleaning, doing laundry, cooking, baking, and making sure her yard was pretty. She probably even had a to-do list to keep all of her tasks on track. Many of us can relate to Martha. She knew what needed to be done and wanted to be hospitable.

Mary, Martha's sister, wasn't bothered by the dishes in the sink. She wasn't concerned about the preparations for Jesus' visit. Mary was only focused on spending quality time with the Lord.

When Jesus, the sister's special guest, arrived, Martha was tired of doing all of the work by herself. She desperately pleaded for Jesus to tell Mary to come and help her!

"As Jesus and his disciples were on their way, he came to a village where a woman named Martha opened her home to him. She had a sister called Mary, who sat at the Lord's feet listening to what he said. But Martha was distracted by all the preparations that had to be made. She came to him and asked, 'Lord, don't you care that my sister has left me to do the work by myself? Tell her to help me!'" -Luke 10:38-40 (NIV)

Jesus responded to Martha in a way that was powerful and convicting.

"'Martha, Martha,' the Lord answered, 'you are worried and upset about many things, but few things are needed—or indeed only one. Mary has chosen what is better, and it will not be taken away from her.'" -Luke 10:41-42 (NIV)

I'm sure Martha was shocked. She was the one preparing for Jesus, and He said Mary had chosen what was better.
How are we doing with choosing what is better?

- Choosing what is better looks like reading God's Word in the mornings before we check our phones.
- Choosing what is better looks like writing a sweet card for a friend or sending an encouraging message instead of taking a nap.
- Choosing what is better looks like making quality time with family a priority over personal hobbies.
- Choosing what is better looks like giving our time, talents, and gifts each Sunday when it's tempting to "let other's do it."
- Choosing what is better looks like putting God first in our actions and not just in our words.

What does *choosing what is better* look like in your life?
The purpose of choosing what is better is to live for something today that will make a difference for eternity.
Life is such a special and exciting gift God has given to us. Each second we're alive, there's a purpose for our lives. We weren't made for ourselves, material possessions, or significant others. We were made for God. We were made to know Him, love Him, and bring others to Him. Everything else our Father gives us in life is just extra.

I've been reminded that small daily compromises add up to huge downfalls. Our hearts have to be rooted in Christ daily. Our daily bread is our personal time with Jesus. The Bible mentions daily bread quite often. In Exodus 16:4, God said for the Israelites to gather their food only for the day they were living in. They weren't allowed to store up food for the week ahead.

"Then the Lord said to Moses, 'I will rain down bread from heaven for you. The people are to go out each day and gather enough for that day. In this way I will test them and see whether they will follow my instructions." -Exodus 16:4 (NIV)

Are you up for a challenge?

1. Instead of planning, let's sit at the Planner's feet
2. Let's put God first with our actions and not just in our words
3. Decide what choosing better looks like for you
4. Strive to choose what is better every moment of your life
5. Invest into spending quality time with God daily and receiving your Daily Bread from Him

THE GAME OF LIFE
JUNE 20, 2017

"Stay on the bag! Stay where you are at" shouted the coach to his player. The player was on a mission to reach home plate but needed guidance in getting there.

A game of baseball reflects the game of life we are all in.

We have a Coach.

Jesus knows the game of life we are in. He knows which plays are wise and which ones are not. His desire is to train us, give us direction, and watch us succeed. *We must know, trust, and listen to His voice.*

We have team mates.

Team mates train, practice, win, lose, celebrate, and work *together*. A team is a group rather than an individual. *It takes everyone working together and being united for a victory to take place.*

We only have a certain amount of time in the game of life.

When the game of life is over, we can't change the end result. We have to make the most of the time we have been given. *We have to train and prepare even when it's uncomfortable.* Our ears must be tuned into hearing our Coach's voice. *He gives us clues on what to do and where to go next.* Through hard times and practice, we become better. We must not give up. Our team needs us, and our goal is to slide across the ultimate home plate with the victory.

We have a crowd watching us.

The crowd watching us is made up of opponents and supporters. Our opponents are equally (if not more) prepared than we are to win. They have a coach as well but a different game plan. Their bleachers are full of an audience cheering them on. They want to win just as bad as we do.

Our bleachers are full of family, friends, and loved ones. They see our game of life in a different perspective than we do. They are older and wiser than we are. They support us, share in our joy, and remind us that our work is important.

We have many voices shouting at us.

While on the field and playing the game, there are many voices shouting different comments at us. *We must ignore the voices behind us and focus on the Voice of our Coach in front of us.*

Fellow team mate, your Coach hasn't given up on you. Even if you have missed some practices, God is still longing to teach you new things. Practice and discipline may be rough, but it is making you into a stronger player. There's a purpose for you being placed on the team you're on. Keep showing up to practice and keep working hard. Continue to listen for your Coach's voice. God loves you with an unending love. He chases after you when you're lost and confused. He is proud to call you His child. God has plans to prosper you. He has His best in store for your life. Keep being faithful. Let's give this game of life all we have and cross home plate with the victory.

FORWARD CONFERENCE 2017

JUNE 27, 2017

Hillsong United, Free Chapel, and Bethel Music lead around 13,000 young people and leaders in worship this past weekend. Pastor Reggie Dabbs, Joel Houston, Jentezen Franklin, Chad Veach, Ben Prescott, and Christine Cain deposited so much truth from God's Word into young souls. An arena in Georgia was overflowing with hearts hungry for God's Presence. We were moved by His Spirit, encouraged in our faith, and inspired to live so contagiously for God. Forward Conference is led by Pastor Jentezen Franklin, his family, and his church, Free Chapel. They have a heart for our generation and invest time, talent, and wisdom into equipping us for building God's Kingdom.

Let me tell you about our trip and what God did!

Reggie Dabbs and others reminded us that *Forward Conference is not just a conference. It is a movement.* The conference was where we were fed and inspired to reach the lost. We were called to use what we experienced to make a difference in our homes, schools, churches, and friendships.

Joel Houston, who sings in Hillsong United, spoke Thursday night. His message resonated deep within me. I related to his personal struggles and realized how the enemy attacks us where we are really most strong. Joel Houston loved to skate board as a child, but his parents pushed him to take music lessons. Practicing was definitely not his favorite thing to do. Since Joel's childhood, Joel has been used to lead millions in glorifying God through worship music.

Here are some points from Joel's message:

- "The darkness is a canvas for God to reveal His light"
- **Never put a limit on what God can do in and through you**
- The gift God has given you is more than enough
- Don't waste the gifts God has placed inside your hands
- Don't allow insecurities to hold you back from the things God has in store for your life
- Don't throw away your gift
- God doesn't need us but He wants us
- God will give us everything we need to do exactly what He calls us to do
- God wants *all* of you just the way you are

Reggie Dabbs warned us as he said, "Don't let fear keep you from your destiny". He also emphasized the importance of our choices. He said, "Insignificant choices are really life changing!".

Pastor Jentezen Franklin is a man full of Godly wisdom. He connected stories from the Bible in a way that was fresh and new. He powerfully stated that **"The enemy always targets who and what God is going to use."**

There are many rocks in the Bible we should notice. In Luke 19:40, Jesus proclaimed, "'I tell you,' he replied, 'if they keep quiet, the stones will cry out.'"

1. Jacob's Rock- Genesis 28:18
- God can give you an anointed dream for your life
- Exodus 17:6- God can bring a river to your desert
- God makes a way when there is no way
- Praise God in the small things and watch Him do big things
2. Joshua's Rock- Joshua 6:20
- Walls of resistance cannot stand when someone praises The Lord

- Walls still fall when God's people cry out
3. David's Rock(s)- 1 Samuel 17:40-51
- When you are in the river, God is working on your rough edges
- The Shepherd hand-picked you out of the mud
- God puts you into a sling and releases you into your destiny
- Giants still fall
- **Just as the enemy has a genealogy of giants, the church has to be producing giant slayers**
4. Legion's Rock- Mark 5:5-13
- God killed the spirit of suicide and self-hatred
5. Adulterous Woman's Rock(s)- John 8:1-11
- **Jesus is a stone mover. He is not a stone thrower**
- *You can't change the past, but you can make wise and God honoring decisions today*

The Mess in the Middle was the title of Pastor Chad Veach's sermon. He preached about the story of Samson found in Judges 14-16.

- Samson was destined for greatness
- Samson was distracted by weakness
- **Don't just know the calling on your life. Fulfill the calling God has on your life**
- **The enemy knows that you are a threat to him**
- Samson was determined for redemption

I loved hearing, learning from, and being inspired by Pastor Ben Prescott. He said:

- We can't miss our calling by being focused on the training
- God says, "If you go, I will show"
- The calling on your life is uncommon and is going to require faith
- Flee from evil and cling to what is good (Romans 12:9)
- There is power in what you flee and cling to
- If we do something that's supernatural, it draws people to God Who lives within us
- The call of God comes in a quiet place
- David's call did not come when He was King. David's call came when he was a shepherd
- Moses was not called in front of all the Israelites. Moses was called in the desert
- The enemy only goes after those most threatening to him
- **One of the greatest things the enemy uses is tricking us to settle for less than God's best**
- There is a higher calling on your life
- **The enemy isn't after you. He is after the calling on your life. The calling on your life doesn't just affect you. The calling on your life is strong enough to touch millions of lives and change the world!**
- There is safety in wise counsel (Proverbs 11:14)
- The call of God on your life has nothing to do with you
- Life is about taking the Kingdom of God to those in need of Him
- We have to be more hungry for the touch of God than anything else

Mrs. Christine Cain brought truth to us in our last service. She spoke on shame, and how God never intended for us to know what shame feels like

(Genesis 2:25). She is passionate about people finding life in Christ so that they can set others free.

- Jesus shamed shame on the cross
- You have to know Whose you are
- Build your life on the truth of God's Word
- Don't elevate any other voice above God's voice

This trip was not only spiritually rewarding but relational as well. The laughs my friends and I shared while traveling were priceless. We sang, dreamed, shared goals, were ourselves, joked, snacked, and grew closer to each other while digging deeper into the love God has for each of us. I'm thankful for all the experiences God has used to make me into who I am today. I'm also more full of passion to spread the love of Jesus with those who are lost. We have a Father Who loves us with all He has. I pray we all come before God humbly and serve Him with the lives He has given to us.

BORN TO STAND OUT

JULY 15, 2017

"I don't fit in at school" whispered my little cousin. She realized she was different but didn't know it was a good thing.

Do you find yourself standing out more than fitting in? Are you struggling to keep up with the latest trends and constantly feeling pressure to be in a relationship?

We all face and have to fight these thoughts. When they creep into our minds, we have to commit them to God and fill ourselves up with His truth.

You have been created by the King of Kings and Lord of Lords. The Creator of the Universe is your Daddy. What He thinks and says about you is more important than anything else. His blood washes over you. You are forgiven in His name. You don't have to keep walking in shame or guilt. God has called you to live in His freedom. He knew every decision you'd make before you were born. Jesus chose to die for you knowing the times you'd hurt Him. He finds so much joy in redeeming you. *You were called to do much more than obsess over social media, seek love in lust, and try to keep up with standards that are temporary and fleeting.*

If you're not fitting in, you're actually in the right spot. That means you aren't like those around you. Instead, you are reflecting your Heavenly Father. More than anything else, you're constantly striving to be made more in His image. You're a rare jewel. You are set apart. You're gifted in a unique way to change this world for our Father's glory. You are beautiful, loved, and worthy of Jesus' blood.

If you find yourself standing out instead of fitting in, you're making God proud. You're making a difference with your life. Keep being different. God calls us to stand out and shine bright. Our faith should be more than evident in everything we say, think, touch, and do.

I challenge you to:

1. Be the one who walks away from what is wrong
2. Be the one who doesn't settle for less
3. Be the one with high standards and God-sized dreams
4. Be the one who takes the road less traveled

"Enter through the narrow gate. For wide is the gate and broad is the road that leads to destruction, and many enter through it. But small is the gate and narrow the road that leads to life, and only a few find it." -Matthew 7:13-14 (NIV)

HOW TO FIND YOUR GIFTS

JULY 21, 2017

Gifts come wrapped in paper, bags, and bows. **Only the Giver of the gift knows what's been placed inside of something until the gift is unwrapped.** Gifts are special. They come from loved ones. They are usually things we long for and enjoy.

I'm sure you are familiar with the gifts others have. You're convinced the girl in first period never hits the snooze button in the mornings. She always seems to be cheerful and full of joy. Your cousin can sing better than people on TV. Your sibling makes straight A's without ever studying. You're always hearing and seeing the good things other people have and thrive in. Perhaps you question if, maybe, there's something special within you as well.

Let me tell you, friend, that there's a spark within you. It was placed there by God when He created you. He has a detailed plan on using your gifts to change the world for His glory.

Gifts are most special when wrapped up. It is fun and exciting for God to watch you unwrap what He has hidden deep inside of you. He wants to see your reaction to discovering your gift! He will pay attention to how you use it.

"Where your deep gladness meets the world's deep sadness" is another way to describe gifts. They're things that bring us joy, excitement, and passion.

How can you find and discover your gifts?

1. Reflect on your childhood.

What did you enjoy doing as a child? God created the gifts He'd give us before the creation of the World. He isn't going to wait until we're old to start stirring them within us. Jesus starts developing our gifts within us when we are young. Did you enjoy playing school, feeding and mothering dolls or stuffed animals, interacting with other kids at church, singing at VBS, or attempting to play an instrument? Pay attention to what brought you joy as a child!

2. Rid your life of distractions.

What are you feeding yourself? *We overflow with what we fill ourselves up with.* To hear God's voice, we need to be seeking Him through His Word, prayer, and Godly counsel. Unhealthy relationships and focuses can hinder us in loving and serving God fully. We have to make sure we are choosing what is better.

3. Realize what you have that others need.

There are so many broken and hurting people. You never know what your word of encouragement, kind conversation, song, strength, story, finances, or friendship may mean to them. As I was reminded at the Youth Theology Institute, we need to approach every day with divine appointments.

God has given us hope so we can help others. He has given us trials so we can teach others about triumphs.

Gifts are meant to be used to reach people for God's kingdom. They aren't limited to leadership, teaching, serving, photography, singing, or athletics. There are millions of gifts that God has created and given. Each one is equally important and unique. Don't compare your gift to the person beside you. Find your spark, grow and develop it, and be amazed by how God uses it.

YOUNG AND BEARDLESS

AUGUST 4, 2017

Young and Beardless by John Luke Robertson inspired me to be more adventurous, go after my dreams, and live fearlessly in my relationship with God.

Listed below are some of my most favorite thoughts from the book:

- "Before you start heading toward a destination, you have to know where you're starting from."
- "When we try to fit into a box by being a personality we think others want to see, we rob ourselves of being confident in who we really are."
- "Dreaming is a gift given to each of us."
- "You don't have to have a plan. You just have say yes to the plan God has for you."
- "Because the people who are crazy enough to think they can change the world, are the ones who do."
- "He told me that the best definition for a vision is having a highly detailed mental picture of a preferable future."
- "Dreams often start in simple places. They're often born out of joy and hope."
- "When a dream starts from the right place, God will surely bless it."
- "When you announce a dream, you give it a chance to live in a world outside your own head."

- "And never forget: dreams that change the world aren't always big dreams, and they don't always require money."
- "God calls us to be with people, even if we don't know why. Sometimes the "impact" is just being there."
- "God never expects perfection. He just expects you to try."
- "The first step was going through the door that had just opened."
- "Before taking a leap of faith, we need to make sure our plans line up with what God wants us to do."

"Sometimes our encounters with others are brief. But no matter the window of time you have together, you can show that person God's love, because God's love can live in the smallest of actions."

BE STILL AND KNOW

AUGUST 15, 2017

I have honestly not been looking forward to starting school next Monday. I've been clinging onto each moment of summer and the familiarity of the current season I'm in. Change is on the horizon and quickly approaching me.

God has been opening and closing doors.

The last part of Revelation 3:7 (NIV) says, "What he opens no one can shut, and what he shuts no one can open."

One of my closest friends is about to move and continue in ministry as a result of Jesus working on his behalf, many prayers being answered, and seasons of preparation finally being completed.

I'm about to start my junior year in high school.

Liberty University is going to have me for a weekend in September.

My family's home is getting some new floors.

My little sister will be joining me in high school and the groups I'm involved in.

Our youth group is being relaunched with a new name and a new mission.

Change may look different for each of us. It is sometimes hard, but it is always necessary. *I've learned that change stretches us and usually results in growth.*

Instead of being overwhelmed by the unknown of this next season, I'm asking Jesus to fill my mind with His beautiful truths. He holds each chapter of our lives and has a divine plan for each one of them. God has already walked our next steps.

"He says, 'Be still, and know that I am God; I will be exalted among the nations, I will be exalted in the earth.'" -Psalm 46:10

As I sat in Jesus' Presence, I felt Him speak the following words to me:

"Be still and know that I am God. You don't need to work so hard trying to gain My attention. I never change. While everything around you is changing, I remain constant. I have a plan for you along with your brothers and sisters in Me that's full of life, growth, joy, and service. Trials will come, but just keep seeking Me as your *highest priority.* I'm living within and through you. You never walk alone. Each breath you breathe, I'm working on your behalf. Stop running and doing and start *being* aware of Who I am and where I dwell. Nothing apart from Me truly matters. I go before you. There's no need for you to worry. Rest in the peace of My Presence. I know what I'm doing. Trust Me. Seek Me. Share your every thought, desire, and care with Me. Bring Me the things you hide. *There's no need to walk in shame when I've set you free. You are free indeed.* There's nothing in all Creation that can separate you from Me. I treasure you. I have the best in store for you. Put Me first with your actions. The enemy is out to devour you. Be aware of the war that takes place. You are a warrior instead of a worrier. I've already defeated the devil, My child. You aren't limited in My Presence. Let Me give you My best. Will you let go of the things I have another plan for? I know your heart. I created the desires you have. Be still and know I'm fighting for you. Be still and know you're My child. Live like you believe these things. Expose the darkness with Light."

Let's be still and know Who God is. Let's not underestimate His power or plans. Let's be determined to walk in victory daily. Let's serve others selflessly. Be encouraged in truth today, friend!

Walking in victory,

Haley

KNOW WHO YOU'RE FIGHTING

SEPTEMBER 9, 2017

Spiritual warfare is no joke. The enemy is constantly seeking to devour God's children.

Sometimes we have to literally remind the enemy that we're not afraid of him. We have already overcome him and his army because of Jesus' power that lives within us.

Read the following words as a victory song:

Devil,

You know your time is more limited than mine is. I am clothed in Light. Light Himself lives within me. I will never be shaken. You are a liar. You kill, steal, and destroy. You are pitiful to say the least. You're weak, but my God is strong. My God has already defeated you, death, hell, and the grave. Hallelujah!

You are busy and up to no good. Good does not exist in you. You do not have authority. You do not have power over my mind, heart, or life. *Just so you're aware, I cheer Jesus on as He kicks you in the teeth.* You have no stronghold on my life or in my home. Flee. Right now. You know what's coming. The Name of Jesus. The name of Jesus makes mountains jump. Jesus' name turns darkness into light. Jesus' name provides safety and peace. Jesus' name is a tower, refuge, and shield.

Just a warning, enemy, know Who you are messing with. It's not me. It's not my family or my friends. You're messing with the One and only Lord Almighty! At His name, you flee. You're kicked in the teeth. You fall. You stand defeated. *You lose the battles you fight because my Jesus has already won!*

This is your warning. I will not tolerate you. You will not plant weeds in my mind, life, or home.

I stand victoriously forgiven, redeemed, chosen, worthy, called, and dearly loved by God.

I already know Jesus is and will continue to use my life to help lost people find true Light and Life in Him. I do not play for your team, enemy. Just so you know Who you're messing with, it's not me. My Daddy is my Shield and my Defender. Jesus comforts and carries me when I am weak. He is my song of peace. He has carried me this far and will forever go before me.

Just so you know Who you're messing with, it's not me. You're powerless, Satan. My Father uses the things you intend for evil to accomplish His many purposes for good. Heaven is my home. While my body has breath in it, I'm changing this World for God's glory. Jesus is my Strength, Protector, and Shield. You're fighting against the One Who has already won.

THE 40 DAY PRAYER CHALLENGE

SEPTEMBER 19, 2017

People read books more often than they meet authors.

In Day 2 of his book *Draw the Circle*, Mark Batterson says, "The right book in the right hands at the right time can save a marriage, avert a mistake, plant a seed, conceive a dream, solve a problem, and prompt a prayer."

God opened my eyes to a special reality after reading that quote. Just as a writer is the true force behind a book, God is the true force behind us! Jesus is the Creator, Artist, and Writer behind everything that has ever existed, is existing, or will ever exist.

As humans, we are made in God's image. The King of the World gave us His characteristics. We were created *on purpose for a purpose* by God.

Because we are His, we are living books pointing others to our Author.

Readers can learn more about our Author through the way we live our lives.

Are we emitting and overflowing with God's light?

Are the pages of our lives reflecting our Author?

THE BACKSTORY OF MY WEEKEND AT LIBERTY

OCTOBER 2, 2017

God is the most detailed Planner of all time! Nothing is a coincidence when God is on the move! My Heavenly Father took countless pieces of a puzzle and hand picked where each one would connect. I just imagine the joy radiating through Him and the smile on His face as I kept watching Him open doors for my weekend at Liberty!

Four years ago, I met a girl named Natalie at FUGE camp in the mountains of North Carolina. I was thirteen years old going into eighth grade. At the time, I was struggling with finding my identity in temporary things and needing freedom from some unhealthy relationships. It was my first time attending FUGE camp, and I LOVED each second of it!

At FUGE camp, campers sign up for tracks which are activities they will do each day. I was in a painting and peer evangelism track. On the first day of the painting track, everyone was put into groups. My group included two other girls, one guy, and myself. One of the girls (Natalie) and I really connected. We had a lot in common and just instantly bonded.

Each groups' painting was to be sold for missions' money. Natalie's church actually bought our painting! The finished product of our canvas was red with the Earth in the center. A mission statement ("Pray Give Go") was written inside of the Earth and white prints of each of our hands extended towards the Earth.

Although Natalie and I had only met the week of camp and spent a few hours together, we knew God had allowed our paths to cross for a divine purpose. Once camp was over and we were all back home, Natalie and I became pen pals and constantly encouraged one another! During the years between then to now, we dreamed of the day we'd see each other again in person.

I believe God gives us glimpses into the future through nudges.

For some reason (I know it was God), I had a "crazy" thought that maybe- just maybe- Natalie and I would go to the same college one day. God had also given each of us a nudge about Liberty University. We both knew something was special about the school and how it could and would possibly be a huge part of our lives.

Fast forward to the fall of 2017...

I am now a junior in high school and Natalie is a freshman at Liberty University!

The teachers of my school go to Myrtle Beach each year for a conference. While they are gone, students receive a few days out of school! This year's break was September 27-29 along with the weekend!

One of my aunts planned a vacation to Massanutten Virginia at the end of September. She asked my mom if our family would be interested in joining her. Behind the scenes, my mom helped plan our trip to Massanutten while also hoping we could tour Liberty while in Virginia.

Over the summer, I received an email from Liberty regarding a scholarship opportunity. It was called the Unashamed Project. The requirements were to:

-Write a 500-1500 word paper on how you live unashamed for Christ

-Submit the paper by a certain date

-Register for and attend September 28-31 CFAW

-Present your paper to a panel of judges

What the paper asked for was what I had just shared on a television broadcast with Mrs. Elkie Brabble! I remember going into my parent's room and showing them the video with information about the Unashamed Project Scholarship. They also realized this was clearly a door God was leading me through.

*Spoiler Alert: I was not the receiver of the scholarship, but I did gain some things that were even more valuable!

At this point in the story, I was out of school, had Liberty's College for a Weekend, and a scholarship opportunity while my family had a resort to stay at ALL during September 28-31!

God truly blows me away with His goodness and faithfulness!

After finding out I'd be at Liberty for the last weekend in September, I told Natalie! We then found hope in the possibility of me rooming with her! Since she had only been at Liberty around five weeks, she didn't really know what the process required to host a CFAW student.

After checking into Liberty around 2:00 p.m. on Thursday, I received my room assignment with Natalie! My parents, Darby, and I finally made it to the right dorm building after turning around a few times.

Once I found the right room number and knocked lightly on the door, Natalie and I were reunited in person for the first time in four years! After rooming with her, Natalie told me the fact she was able to host me was a God thing in itself!

This story gives God glory for orchestrating every detail for my weekend at Liberty! He is so good! Be encouraged that God's timing truly is better than anything we could ever plan on our own!

Giving thanks,

Haley

THE UNASHAMED PROJECT SCHOLARSHIP

OCTOBER 7, 2017

On the day of the Unashamed Project (September 30, 2017), I woke up around 6:00 in the morning, went into the community dorm bathroom, listened to God inspired songs, and got ready.

After putting away my beauty bag, pajamas, and other essentials, I exited the doors of the dorm building. The air outside was very crisp. Sitting underneath a shade tree on a picnic table, I read verses of encouragement, ate four orange "nab" crackers, drank some water, messaged my family, and made my way down steps that led to a main walkway to buildings. My little fall booties were boldly making noise each step I took towards the Jerry Falwell Library where the Unashamed event started.

When I got to the library, a fellow Unashamed participant held the door open for me. We began to talk about our papers, jittery thoughts, and curious questions. Not knowing anyone else participating in the scholarship contest, Chase and I chose to stay together during the process. Although we heard different numbers, we are quite confident around 300 juniors and seniors intended on participating in the project. Only an estimated 250 students showed up on the big day of presenting our papers!

As Chase and I were in line to check in, we turned around to see another brother in Christ who quickly completed our new friend group. We comforted, encouraged, prayed with, and supported one another!

"TLGSTHP TLBHPWP Ps 29:11" was written on my hand. As I am sure it looked like another language or secret code (lol), Ethan asked what the letters stood for. I was then able to share Psalm 29:11 (NIV), a verse I was clinging onto, with him. It says "The Lord gives strength to his people; the Lord blesses his people with peace."

We all checked in, received our room assignments and times, grabbed a bottle of juice or cup of coffee, and found our own little bench/backless couch to sit on. For about two hours, we just sat there and bonded. We had just met each other for the first time, but our spirits connected on a level created and understood by God Almighty. He knew each of us individually and worked in miraculous ways to intersect our paths. Chase, Ethan, and I truly felt God's love as our "family reunion" took place. We each walked into the library physically by ourselves but walked out as a strand of three cords that was not easily broken (Ecclesiastes 4:12).

Chase and I were assigned rooms inside the Demoss building while Ethan was assigned a room in the library. Before we headed into two different directions, we all took turns praying together and exchanged phone numbers to stay connected throughout the day.

I found my assigned room in Demoss and didn't wait any more than five minutes before I was called in to present my paper. In a small classroom, two judges were extremely intentional with the few minutes they had with me. They asked me questions to see my heart on a level deeper than the surface. They also prayed with me before even asking that I present my paper! Given the option to stand up or sit down, I chose to sit down as they asked me to be more conversational in sharing the details of my story. They were sitting down as well. As I spoke, I was overwhelmed with emotion remembering the miracles God has done in and through my life! Even though this scholarship opportunity was huge,

God had placed a peaceful wave of His boldness within me. He had opened countless doors and made a way for me to be at Liberty the weekend of September 28-October 1, 2017. I talked with the judges and completed my presentation in about ten minutes. Afterwards, I called my mom and checked on Chase and Ethan. They still had not been called in to present their papers.

After everyone was finished with the first round, we all met back up at the library! We headed towards the rot (dining hall), but decided to enjoy the beautiful fall weather by going on top of Demoss! It was around 12:00 in the afternoon. The view and atmosphere on the roof of Demoss is one of my favorite things about Liberty! We then headed towards the bookstore to look around in there. Our hungry stomachs quickly led us towards the rot, where we ate food from a place like Chipotle. The anticipation was heavy as we prepared to find out the results of round one. Apparently, around twenty-five people out of the original 250 made it to round two! Rushing towards the TV, everyone was frantically searching for their name. Chase and Ethan, who were taller and closer to the TV than I was, searched for my name. Ethan and I made it into round two! We didn't have time to sit and talk like the previous round so we headed back into Demoss. After helping each other find our rooms, we embarked on round two! The day was honestly tiring but so rewarding! For the second round, we were in different classrooms with two different judges. Mine were college or grad students. My presentation went well but a little faster than the first time. Overall, it still went very well. Ethan was the last person to present in his assigned room.

The results for round three were the most nerve-racking! The remaining estimated twenty-five of us went inside of a conference meeting type room back inside of the library. That was where the five finalists were announced! Although I wasn't a finalist, Ethan was!

The girl who won the scholarship ministers through Spoken Word poems. After praying that God's will be done, I rest in the fact that His plans are far greater than anything I could ever imagine on my own. I was joyful and am still so overwhelmed by having the opportunity to be a part of a movement of living unashamed for my Heavenly Father. He brought two new friends into my life and poured out His Holy Spirit upon us. We spoke with courage, confidence, and boldness. We reflected on the miracles God had done in and through us. We were inspired to keep praying and seeing miracles.

Living unashamed for Jesus isn't about writing or presenting a paper to win a scholarship. Rather, living unashamed for Jesus is done when we think no one else is looking. Living unashamed, to me, means being intentional with each breath God gives to me. No one is perfect, but we are all called to a higher purpose in this life. Our lives are not about us.

LEAVING COMFORT
OCTOBER 8, 2017

Comfort.

It's found in our homes, families, big sweaters, food, social media pages, and many other things. Where do you find your comfort?

God did miraculous things in, through, for, and around me my freshman year of high school. While that is a wonderful season to reflect upon, I have to be seeking and seeing Jesus where He is working now. God wants to show Himself to me in new ways.

Change is something that scares and excites me.

My youth group was recently relaunched! We rebranded and renamed two of our ministries, changed the background of our stage, and started small group circles.

I think a lot of us miss out on God's best by clinging onto what we think is good.

How dare we stay inside our comfort zones of ordinary when God has called us to live extraordinary lives of impact, courage, boldness, and mission? We should never be comfortable with where we are at in our relationships with God. We should constantly be seeking to discover *more* of God to grow closer to Him.

God has given me a book to write. He has given me a mouth to speak. How am I living out these callings given to me by God? What is God calling you to do?

I challenge us to not only read our Bibles but to pray as well. **A relationship without communication is nonexistent.** While Jesus is King of the World, He is also our personal best friend. Sharing our thoughts and hearts with God daily increases our intimacy with Him.

Stop living under the trap of comparison. God loves you with every part of His being. Let's not get immune to His goodness or hearing of His love for us.

Application:

- Be more intentional about my prayer life daily.
- Grow the seeds God has placed within me.
- Do what God is calling me to do!
- Rid my life of comfort and things that distract me from God.

FIGHTING FEAR

OCTOBER 27, 2017

Fear chokes out freedom.

On the outside, your life may seem as perfect as it can be; but on the inside, there's something holding you back from true life and freedom. The struggle within you is seen by God. He knows the anxious thoughts that pass through your mind. It hurts His heart to see you fight fear.

Waking up to a growing feeling of panic and anxiety was a part of my freshman year of high school. The enemy tortured my mind. A fear of quietness and stomach noises held me in chains. I was praying for freedom, peace, and a breakthrough every day. The lies and fear of the enemy was affecting every decision I made. It limited the things I felt comfortable doing. Mental health cannot be ignored. Our thoughts affect every other aspect of our lives!

On the outside, others saw me handing out cards and cookies. They saw me with Impact Bible Study praying. My classmates associated me with joyful smiling. My inward battle of fighting fear was not known to many of my peers. **We may try to hide our struggles with smiles, but God sees the real issues we are facing within.**

Let me tell you why the enemy chooses to fight you so hard and so often, my friend.

1. You are the apple of God's eye

God's children are His most prized possessions. My youth pastor, Matt Hart, said the enemy attacks us, God's children, because that's the only way he can touch God. The devil knows it breaks God's heart when humans don't accept God's gift of salvation.

2. Your calling does not just affect you

Your calling will impact millions of lives and stir revival among the nations. Pastor Ben Prescott reminded me of this at the Forward Conference.

3. The Power Source within you reminds the enemy of his destiny

God is taking back His people who were once lost. The enemy's kingdom is temporary and forever shaken. When you lie down in peace and rise with joy, the devil knows God is on the move through you.

Philippians 2:10-11 (CSB) should bring so much comfort to those of us who belong to God. It exclaims, "so that at the name of Jesus every knee will bow—in heaven and on earth and under the earth—and every tongue will confess that Jesus Christ is Lord, to the glory of God the Father."

At the name of Jesus, the enemy bows and confesses that Jesus Christ is Lord!

God broke each chain that once held me captive. The enemy has no power over my life. God's peace flows from my mind to my feet.

Brother or sister, you are not alone in this battle. **I know it may be hard to believe it, but *today* is the day for you to find freedom!** *Fighting fear does not mean your life is not right with God.* Most likely, you are fighting fear because God is using your life to shake this World up for His glory. **It is not a sin to be tempted to fear. Instead, it is a sin when we choose to live in fear.**

It is never God's desire for you to live in fear or to suffer in any way. We face trials because the World we live in is fallen due to sin.

The process of being healed is not always how or when we think it will be. Rather, it will be in God's perfect timing.

In 2 Kings 5, a man named Naaman sought to be healed from his leprosy. His journey to being healed was different from what he expected it to be. Instead of being cured by the prayers of Elisha instantly, Naaman was told to wash himself in the Jordan River seven times.

2 Kings 5:9-15 (NIV) says, "So Naaman went with his horses and chariots and stopped at the door of Elisha's house. Elisha sent a messenger to say to him, 'Go, wash yourself seven times in the Jordan, and your flesh will be restored and you will be cleansed.' But Naaman went away angry and said, 'I thought that he would surely come out to me and stand and call on the name of the Lord his God, wave his hand over the spot and cure me of my leprosy. Are not Abana and Pharpar, the rivers of Damascus, better than all the waters of Israel? Couldn't I wash in them and be cleansed?' So he turned and went off in a rage. Naaman's servants went to him and said, 'My father, if the prophet had told you to do some great thing, would you not have done it? How much more, then, when he tells you, 'Wash and be cleansed'!' So he went down and dipped himself in the Jordan seven times, as the man of God had told him, and his flesh was restored and became clean like that of a young boy. Then Naaman and all his attendants went back to the man of God. He stood before him and said, 'Now I know that there is no God in all the world except in Israel. So please accept a gift from your servant.'"

Sweet friend,

The trial you're going through, whether it's fighting fear or another battle, has already been won by God. You have victory through His blood and Name. I can promise you that God desires to use this part of your testimony to uplift and speak life into others who will be fighting the same battle you're currently facing.

Genesis 50:20 (NIV) says, "You intended to harm me, but God intended it for good to accomplish what is now being done, the saving of many lives."

What the enemy intends for evil, God uses for good. Good for you and countless other people as well!

LIVE ORIGINAL TOUR 2017

NOVEMBER 6, 2017

One of my mom's friends, Mrs. Jenny, planned a trip to the Live Original Tour in Myrtle Beach. She kindly invited my family to attend with her family and youth group! About a week after my family was invited, my mom casually told me about it. She did not even realize it was the same tour I had been talking about for a few years! God is so good to us! *He doesn't just know the desires of our hearts. He acts upon them.*

God has been depositing some things within me, and I want to share them with you.

"I am calling you to places no one else wants to go. Places that aren't safe or clean. My people need Me. I live inside of you and I am the Hope of the World. I am calling you to places no one else wants to go. Other people may not understand this purpose I have given you. That is okay. You know clearly I have called you to this. *My Presence is found in the most broken places. My joy is transparent in the face of destruction and loss.* My children know My voice, and they follow after Me. I have not called **you** to an ordinary life of comfort. Drop the masks. *Strive for excellence instead of perfection.* I delight in you, My child. Are you delighting in Me alone? *Does the way you live your life testify that I am enough for you?* Do not be seeking Me in worthless and temporary things. *Stop doing and start being.* Focus on Me."

Jesus has been reminding me of His friendship. He is not just my Creator and Father. He is my best friend. *God wants His very best for me, and He doesn't let me settle for anything less.*

I had another moment that reminded me why I am living this past weekend. God whispered, "Don't you see now why you do not need to settle for what's familiar? Look at this. This is what I have made you for. Planning conferences, speaking, writing books, and using all of your gifts to bring Me glory and to build My kingdom."

Also…

"Wait patiently for the fearless, bold, passionate and called man of Me who I have to be your husband. Do not worry about him. I know him intimately. He is My son. Just keep your eyes on Me, daughter. Run after Me as hard as you can. Pray with everything within you. Do not try to figure out the roles people play in your life. I will make Myself and My plans known. Your future husband is loving and serving Me. You keep doing the same. Each of you were not made for each other. Both of you were made for Me. I delight in each of you and know how much more effective you will be in My kingdom together. I will bring you together in My timing.

Ditch religion and dive into your personal relationship with Me. Mark your Bible up. Meditate on each verse. Pray with passion and intensity. Persevere through each trial. Dream even bigger God-sized dreams."

FRESHNESS OVER FAMILIARITY

NOVEMBER 15, 2017

There is so much of God that we have yet to discover because we have limited faith.

Limited faith sometimes looks like going to church, serving with all of our free time, and reading prayer books while also neglecting personal intimacy with our Father. Pastor Christian Powell said, *"Time spent with God is more important than time spent for God."*

God is actually more concerned about our hearts than our efforts. When we seek God for who He is, not for what we can get, He reveals Himself to us in such deep and personal ways.

Doing things for the kingdom of God is a result of being in the Presence of God. We cannot pour Truth into others if we, ourselves, are empty of Truth.
The devil knows how powerful our time with God is. God loves to give and reveal His dreams and plans to us. He shares hints of my future to me. I am reminded that *I am very weak on my own, but with Christ, I am unstoppable.*

God does not want fancy prayers and perfectly positioned quiet times from us. He already knows our deepest hurts and desires. *He is with us in the messiness.* During the hardest season of my life, Christ saw purpose in me. He knew I needed help. Jesus wasn't afraid of the process of restoring my mind and heart. He never pushed me away. Instead, He constantly came after me. God *worked on my behalf even when I didn't ask Him to.*

Jesus is not confined to our coffee cups and wall art sayings. God is breathing. He is living in an amazing amount of people, places, and things.

Are our to-do lists and busy schedules limiting the power of God in our lives? We must take a deep look into ourselves, our priorities, and where we are giving our time.

As Dale Delaney said, **"Less is more."** While listening to his *Stress is Bad* sermon, God did a work in my heart. Recently, I have been giving myself and my time to different committees at school, my siblings, my parents, my grades, my photography business, and my ministries. Along with all of those things, I have been reading God's Word but challenged to love God with freshness over familiarity.

Dale, being used by God, said a few things I want to share with you!

1. Apply Scripture to you personally.
2. Are you going to let something define you or are you going to define it?
3. Do not let stress limit your impact in the kingdom of God.
4. Your identity is not based off of what you can do, but what God has already done.
5. If you keep something private, you have no accountability.
6. You are not meant to do life alone.
7. Jesus did not wait for the disciples to come to Him. Jesus went to the disciples Himself. Do not wait for people to come to you before you start mentoring and ministering unto them. You have a responsibility to reach out to people first.
8. Use your past to invest into someone else's future.
9. Flock to Jesus no matter what is going on.
10. Stress is a tool the enemy uses to kill, steal, and destroy. God is and gives Life and Victory.

Whatever you are going through, friend, I pray God meets your need. I pray you see Him for Who He truly is. I pray we will feast upon Him constantly, and be full of His joy.

With love,

Haley

IN CHRIST ALONE

DECEMBER 3, 2017

Hey, friend! I hope you are living abundantly in Christ. Not just surviving, going through your daily routine, tired, and counting down the days until your next break. I look back on the month of November in my planner and stand amazed at the supernatural strength God gave me. My days were booked with trips, photo shoots, school events, church, and family time. All of those things bring me joy, but I can easily struggle to have Christ as my highest priority whenever I am involved in so many different things.

My spirit has recently been attacked in a way I am not used to. I have been fighting darkness in the form of classmates and peers. I am extremely burdened for people I love and care for who are blinded to God's light. Honestly, this spiritual battle has been something the enemy has attempted to use to distract me from living out God's purpose for my life.

We must not listen to the lies of the enemy, my friend. God's plans for our lives are full of hope, love, joy, peace, abundance, life, freedom, victory, and miracles. **With Christ in us, our lives on Earth have the power to change other people's eternities.**

We, as God's children, must not become weary in doing good.

"Let us not become weary in doing good, for at the proper time we will reap a harvest if we do not give up." -Galatians 6:9 (NIV)

Let's get back to dreaming God-sized dreams. Let's get back to praying fervently and passionately. Let's get back to spending time with God each and every day. Let's get back to giving encouragement in various forms. Let's get back to having our priorities in order.

What are some things you need to rearrange in your life? Please listen to me, friend. You are carrying more than what God intends for you to carry. Your weaknesses can be your strengths whenever you give them over to God. I do not write to you as having everything figured out. **What I do know is that Jesus plus nothing is more than what I need.** *Christ alone is my deepest desire, greatest love, best friend, faithful listener, generous giver, and abounding in peace Father.*

God wants us to live in Him which results in living with the fruits of His Spirit. If you are looking for love, accept God. If you are looking for peace, accept God. If you are looking for joy, you are only going to find it in Christ.

On my own, friend, I am weak and broken. Every breath I breathe, I need Jesus. We all need Him to be what we could never be on our own. He is perfect.

In the words of Micah Tyler, "I don't want to trade God's plan for something familiar." I encourage you to go listen to his song *Different*.

Let's remember that only in God are we going to find all we are searching for and all we need.

I love you, brother or sister in Christ, and I am praying God continues to finish His perfect work in your life!

-Haley

RAW ENCOUNTERS

DECEMBER 21, 2017

During my week at North Carolina Wesleyan College for the YTI Program, I saw and experienced Heaven on Earth.

It was past bedtime on a Thursday night whenever my leader realized some students were outside of the dorms. She left our conversation to bring my peers back inside. Instead of getting the students and coming back, Paige stayed outside. I was called to see what was happening and was shocked to find my peers gathered around a gazebo crying out to God! Shouting, praying, tears, conviction, and broken addictions were all around me. My brothers and sisters in Christ were being moved by God's Holy Spirit powerfully. It was dark outside and many people in the dorms were already asleep. We all *should* have been asleep too, but God had a raw encounter planned for us.

Encounters with God are not perfectly packaged, but, instead, fully raw. Encounters with God happen when we least expect them to. They are not tied up with bows and ribbons. They are hidden treasures.

There has never been a night more miraculous than the night Jesus was born.

"And it came to pass in those days, that there went out a decree from Caesar Augustus that all the world should be taxed. (And this taxing was first made when Cyrenius was governor of Syria.) And all went to be taxed, every one into his own city. And Joseph also went up from Galilee, out of the city of Nazareth, into Judaea, unto the city of David, which is called Bethlehem;

(because he was of the house and lineage of David:) To be taxed with Mary his espoused wife, being great with child. And so it was, that, while they were there, the days were accomplished that she should be delivered. And she brought forth her firstborn son, and wrapped him in swaddling clothes, and laid him in a manger; because there was no room for them in the inn. And there were in the same country shepherds abiding in the field, keeping watch over their flock by night. And, lo, the angel of the Lord came upon them, and the glory of the Lord shone round about them: and they were sore afraid. And the angel said unto them, Fear not: for, behold, I bring you good tidings of great joy, which shall be to all people. For unto you is born this day in the city of David a Saviour, which is Christ the Lord. And this shall be a sign unto you; Ye shall find the babe wrapped in swaddling clothes, lying in a manger. And suddenly there was with the angel a multitude of the heavenly host praising God, and saying, Glory to God in the highest, and on earth peace, good will toward men. And it came to pass, as the angels were gone away from them into heaven, the shepherds said one to another, Let us now go even unto Bethlehem, and see this thing which is come to pass, which the Lord hath made known unto us. And they came with haste, and found Mary, and Joseph, and the babe lying in a manger. And when they had seen it, they made known abroad the saying which was told them concerning this child. And all they that heard it wondered at those things which were told them by the shepherds. But Mary kept all these things, and pondered them in her heart. And the shepherds returned, glorifying and praising God for all the things that they had heard and seen, as it was told unto them." -Luke 2:1-20 (KJV)

Jesus chose a young engaged couple to be His earthly parents. His mom who was a virgin was made by Him. Jesus placed His human life inside the hands of a woman He created. He left His royal throne to make His home among brokenness. A palace was not prepared for Jesus' birth. Rather, Jesus was born inside of a stable. His tiny body was placed in a manger. Jesus was and is full of humility. He Who created all people came to Earth to die for their sins.

Innkeepers neglected the opportunity to host the birth of Jesus Christ. They were focused on numbers, making money, and reservations for ordinary people while they rejected the Son of God. *They did not make room for Him because their rooms were already full.*

What do we need to remove from our lives to make room for the King of Kings?

The most miraculous moments happen when we least expect them to.

Are your eyes open to see God? Have you ever experienced a raw encounter with Him? God wants us to be real instead of perfect. He is the only One Who has been or will ever be perfect.

Instead of trying to make things happen on our own, we must listen for God's whispers and be prepared for raw encounters.

God will bring clarity to our chaos, healing to our grief, peace to our storms, and answers to our questions in His own timing. We must seek Jesus as our highest priority and leave our burdens in His hands. God is in us all that we cannot be on our own.

Merry Christmas, my sweet friends! I am praying your days will be filled with praying meaningfully, meditating on God's Word, enjoying family, learning to rest, and having raw encounters with God.

With love,

H

BE

DECEMBER 28, 2017

My spirit feels faint from the constant pressure to do. I feel guilty whenever I sit down on the couch, watch a movie, or do anything unproductive. I realize my time on Earth is limited, and I want to be intentional with the way I use each second.

God created me with a desire to do, but He gave me an even greater need to be.

Instead of cleaning out the few specks of dirt from the towels in my car, God wants my feet to be walking in the woods closer to His heart.

Instead of sitting behind an empty computer screen trying to write a blog post, God wants me to be in His Presence so He can give me His perfect words of encouragement.

Instead of getting anxious about who I will go to prom with, God shows me that His power is unlimited in what He can do in His timing.

Cleaning, writing on my own, anxious thoughts, and all my attempts to do distract me from seeking my Father's face above all.

If I really want to be intentional with my time, I should lay down my idols and run away in quiet time with my Father. **There is a call to be still. There is a command to seek Jesus first. There is a mission we can only accomplish whenever our priorities are in the Father's order.**

If we are doing things only for the sake of doing them, our work will not be blessed.

We can only obediently do whenever we have faithfully been.

What idols are you clinging onto that you need to lay down? What are you currently doing that is actually depleting you of rest and abundant life?

Brother or sister, the devil wants to keep us focused on unimportant things so that our focus will not be on eternal treasures. We must not let him receive a victory from our lives. God did not create us to be as busy as we all are. He created us for Himself, rest, enjoyment, creativity, community, other people, and ministry.

We will be most inspired, blessed, and abundant whenever we choose Jesus over everything else. God's faithful children are His fruitful children.

Listed below are ways I desire to be instead of do. How will you find rest and keep your priorities in the Father's order?

BE IN GOD'S PRESENCE

BE FULL OF JOY

BE A LOVER AND MEDITATOR OF GOD'S WORD

BE ADVENTUROUS

BE KIND, COMPASSIONATE, SELFLESS, AND INTENTIONAL

BE GOAL ORIENTED

BE CONSUMED WITH JESUS

BE GENEROUS

BE HOSPITABLE

BE FULL OF HOPE

BE PURE IN THOUGHTS, DESIRES, MOTIVES, AND ACTIONS

BE THANKFUL AND ENCOURAGING

BE A WOMAN OF PRAYER

THE BEST OF 2017

DECEMBER 29, 2017

While 2017 has been full of life, excitement, joy, and victory, it has also been a year of growth and change.

One of my dad's grandmothers passed away right after we welcomed in 2017. She loved God and her family while she left behind a legacy of contentment.

Darby, my sister, represented her class at school by being on the homecoming court in January. Darby truly sees the best and worst in me. I am closer to her than any other human. We have shared a room since she was two years old and our brother was born. She has found her gifts, developed them, and used them in ministry this year. I could not be more proud of her. Darby has shown love to people who have hurt her, and she constantly exhibits God's grace.

My sweet family, friends, church family, and classmates came together in February to celebrate my sixteenth birthday! The party lasted for a few hours, but it seemed to fly by to me! It was one of the best nights of my life, and I will forever cherish the memories my loved ones and I made.

On the following Monday morning, my mom took me to get my license! We knew where I would have to drive for the test, so I practiced before going to the DMV. Thankfully and excitedly, I passed! Since then my siblings have called me their personal Uber! I have memorized the roads that lead to school, church, home, the grocery store, and a few other places. The guys in my class always joke that I drive slow, which, to them, means going the speed limit or five over!

God used a friend from church to push me closer to Himself and inspire my creativity this year. Jonathan, my brother in Christ, is one of the most Spirit-filled people I have ever met. God has His hand on Jonathan's life, and I have had the honor of seeing God open up doors of opportunity for him. Jonathan always gives his time, talents, and treasure to leave a mark on the world for Jesus. He is a blessing to everyone he meets!

My church, Tanglewood Church of God, is known for the Easter drama it ministers through each year. The Victor is anything but a cute, simple, little Easter drama. Our whole entire church gets involved months before Easter to prepare for the ministry The Victor holds. I do not say that to boast in human strength, but, rather, to marvel at God's goodness! The body of Christ has so many members who are gifted in diverse areas. My dad runs a spot light. My mom serves on the prayer team and on stage. Darby is always involved too. Her role changes from year to year. Remington has had the humbling privilege and responsibility to portray young Jesus. I love on three year olds, take pictures, and experience God's power while being on the prayer team. One of my most favorite Victor memories from this past year included walking in the parking lot while everyone else was in a church building. The sun was setting beautifully, and I was surrounded by hundreds of cars! The cars represented lives, and, most importantly, eternal souls. I held prayer cards inside of my hands and was blessed by being able to pray over them. I cannot even express how much The Victor, the ministry it brings, and my church means to me!

In April, I attended the Grow 1.0 Photography Workshop. The teachers, Jared and Amanda Grantham, taught from their experience on shooting in manual mode. I enjoyed taking what I learned from the class and practicing the skill downtown Goldsboro with a model. I highly recommend the class to photography beginners.

Last Christmas I received a little purple hammock which has been one of my favorite things to enjoy this year, especially in warm weather! Being outside in God's creation makes me feel most alive. My Father shows Himself to me, and I can speak aloud right back to Him.

While my class at school has lost members, we have also gained some new ones. My peers call me MaMa Haley. I cannot help but love them, care about them, and only want what is best for their lives and eternities. I pray for them and am sometimes even burdened to the point of tears for them. I am trying to make the most of the time we have together, which is going by fast!

Remington played baseball in the spring. Since then he has discovered a love for basketball! My family always laughed at his baseball games because daddy would stand with his arms in the air and say, "What are you doing?!". I wish you could hear how he said it. I am thankful Remington has found a sport that he truly enjoys now. He just received a new NIV Bible for Christmas and excitedly keeps telling me what he is reading. There is nothing else that could make me more happy than seeing him walk in Truth.

As my sophomore year of high school was coming to a close, one of my favorite teachers, Mr. Wright, took his art students to downtown New Bern. I went along with them since I participated in the Fine Arts competition. We painted at the Accidental Artist, walked downtown, went into stores and an unusual coffee shop, ate at the Cow Cafe, and ended the day with making some unforgettable memories.

I came down with pneumonia shortly after the field trip.

My photography business really started to take form this year. I have had many sessions and growing opportunities. I am very appreciative of those who let me be a part of their lives by capturing priceless moments. My friend Jonathan, whom I mentioned earlier, is a videographer. He, Ali (a girl from my church), and I took on a wedding together! Ali and I were just there to help Jonathan and learn from having the experience. It was one of the most beautiful weddings I have ever witnessed. I know I've said it before in a post, but we got our own little golf cart to ride and laughed pretty much the whole time we rode it. I'll never forget the Wiggins Wedding!

My cousin Kelsie and her husband Trey had a baby in June! Little Raleigh has been a blessing to our family ever since! I cannot wait to see the ways God uses her life for Himself!

With our youth group, Darby and I went to the Forward Conference in Atlanta Georgia June 22-24. We heard from some of the most sought-after Christian speakers, pastors, and worship leaders. God told me to not limit the ways He could use me.

During last school year, Mrs. Elkie Brabble, one of my mom's friends who hosts a Christian broadcast, contacted me about being on the show! I honestly was surprised but excited for the opportunity to share my testimony and God's faithfulness! We recorded and aired the broadcast in July. Darby came along with me, and I was praying for confidence and peace. God is so so so good! He presents us with opportunities for purposes far greater than ourselves!

One of my sweet kids at VBS, Ainsley, blessed my heart with her fun personality. She always made me laugh. We have stayed in touch since VBS, and I have enjoyed babysitting her and her sister. I love the connections God makes for us!

The United Conference is a student conference that my church has led the past few summers. Helping prepare the venue for the conference this year impacted Darby and I. God used Pastor Daniel Gray to speak specifically to us during one service.

Two of my last favorite memories from this sumner included a beach day with Mrs. Kimmy and Holly and then the Harper family.

God gave me peace about quitting piano lessons for this year and has spoken to my heart about missions.

In the Fall, I went to Liberty University for the very first time! The weekend I was there had God's fingerprints stamped all over it. I saw my friend Natalie for the first time in four years and was able to stay in her dorm with her! God has given me story upon story to show how real and powerful He is! I participated in the Unashamed Project Scholarship and met two new friends and brothers in Christ named Ethan and Chase! I felt like I was in a dream while at Liberty. There is so much I could say about the school and my few days there.

God surprised me with, yet, another gift this year. He made a way for me and my family to go to the Live Original Tour in November! It was such a fun night and weekend full of motivation and encouraged dreams!

My mom and I's "favorite day of the year" is Black Friday. We go by ourselves and get the good deals while Darby has a sleepover with my cousin Taylor! This year, two little kids tried to jump in front of my mom in a line, but she did not let them. I thought it was hilarious!

I am on a mission to finish reading the whole Bible. I have read stories throughout the Bible my whole life, but I want to fully soak up each page of God's Word. I, thankfully, can say I have read the New Testament and have now moved on to working my way through the Old Testament.

God has been speaking to my heart about leading a movement for young women, and I am seeing Him give me the details of it. I will be sharing more information about this with you very soon!

My favorite memory from this Christmas was when my family played Apples to Apples with my cousins Daniel and Temple. We all tried to hint which card was ours, and I even mispronounced a word. That resulted in a lot of laughs!

I am overwhelmed by the love and support God has given to me through you and other people who are living Undeniably His. I have seen God grow the amount of people who read this blog. God receives the glory for anything and everything Undeniably His accomplishes. He is the inspiration and true Writer behind each post. Thank you for giving me accountability and lending an ear to hear how God is working in my life.

2017 has been my most favorite year of life yet, and I absolutely cannot wait to see what is ahead!

What extraordinary things has God shown you or done in your life this year? I would love to lend an ear to hear your stories as well!

Excited for a new year,

Haley

A YEAR OF ENCOUNTERS

2018

LOVE IS PATIENT

JANUARY 29, 2018

Before many of the well-known attributes of love are expressed in 1 Corinthians 13:4-7, love is first described as patient.

The phrase "love is patient" stopped me in my tracks last week and has constantly been brought to my mind daily by God.

I have been praying about who I would go to prom with for over a year now. I placed my love life inside of God's hands before entering ninth grade. Not just physically, but spiritually, mentally, and emotionally as well. I had a mental list of potential people I could ask to go to prom with me, but over the course of a year, God has eliminated each guy by name off of my list. If you had a front row seat of this process, you would be blown away by seeing God work! As He crossed the last person off of my list, I knew God was doing something special behind the scenes of my life. He has constantly reminded me of how big He is. **He has shown me that prayer is my most powerful tool. He has also reconfirmed that nothing can stop or stand in the way of the plans God has for my life. Because God, the Creator of Heaven and Earth is our faithful Father and Friend, we do not have to try to make things happen on our own.**

While I have been tempted to take action on the glimpse of the plan God has revealed to me, I know that without patience, God cannot fully give me His best.

Love is patient and should not only be seen in a romantic way. We are *all* called to live in love and to share love daily because we are all fully and deeply loved by God.

Taking leaps of faith, being patient, and praying like it depends on God is powerful.

God has been doing incredible things in my life this month. I have taken a break from sharing words and pictures on social media in order to give God my undivided attention. While I have been freed from the pressure to constantly post, I have still had to rid my life of distractions.

Another reason I have surrendered some of my most treasured hobbies this month is because I have had my focus on The Delight Movement. It is less than a month away! God has been turning a prophesied dream into a holy reality! He has given me an insurmountable opportunity and responsibility to speak life over teenage girl's lives. Many girls who will come to The Delight Movement will walk through the doors of my church carrying chains I do not know about. My prayer and desire is that God will break the chains of His beloved girls and fully equip them to be *the* change in this dark World that is starving for His light.

While reading about Moses and Aaron in Leviticus, God told me that **a position of leadership never grants a person a membership of perfection.**

God does not use perfect people because perfect people do not exist. Instead, He always uses broken people whom He has set free and restored. We all have sinned and fallen short of the glory of God, yet God has set us apart to live radical lives in and for Him (Romans 3:23). Although God's love for us is not based off of our behavior, I do believe *our acts of faith touch the heart of God.*

Without seasons of preparation, we will never be fully prepared for the plans God has for us. Instead of becoming impatient, I challenge you to rest in the place God has divinely put you. Do not give God a time limit. He Himself is not bound by time. Our minds cannot even fathom the mysteries and miracles God has prepared for us. Keep striving for excellence rather than perfection. Allow God to turn your brokenness into a beautiful message. Do not compare your walk to the run of the girl or the guy beside you. Keep your eyes on the Prize. Never give up but always stop to fill yourself up with Truth so that you can run with endurance.

I am here to be open, honest, and encouraging with you this year!

Much love,

Haley

SEVENTEEN

FEBRUARY 9, 2018

My 365 days of being sixteen have been more than sweet! They have held challenges, hugs, church services, trips of a lifetime, friendships that have awakened my soul, and memories I will always cherish. While being sixteen, I most enjoyed getting my license, driving Valerie (my Volkswagen Beetle), afternoons with my siblings, days in Greenville with my mom and family, beach trips over the summer, gathering loved ones around our kitchen table, Black Friday shopping, church conferences, seeing God grow me personally, and being used by God in ways far greater than I could ever imagine. I have held Jesus' hand and poured my heart out to Him through many walks and talks in the woods. We have accomplished so much together! God has sustained me. He has given me provision for the visions He has placed on my heart. In September, my Father gave me the most special weekend at Liberty University where I stayed with my friend Natalie and participated in the Unashamed Project Scholarship. I have used my freedom in Christ to live fearlessly. I am no longer allowing the enemy to keep me trapped inside a box of uselessness!

I have realized that there is nothing more important in life than our relationships with Jesus and other people. We were not made to do life alone! Life is short. We are not promised tomorrow. Just this week, I have been reminded of that truth. You and I so often take for granted the time and opportunities we have to love others. Instead of pushing our siblings, children, or spouses away, we need to embrace, hug, and cherish them! We need to quit worrying and start living abundantly. Comparison must be quenched in our lives.

God has given each of us a unique mission that only we can fulfill through Him. There are no two humans on Earth who are exactly the same. Every life matters and has value in God. It is easy to become irritated with the people around us who are hard to love, but we are called to go the extra mile to minister unto them. It is easy to judge others, but mercy triumphs over judgment. I have been praying to see others through God's eyes of mercy rather than through fleshly judgment. Synonyms of mercy are compassion, grace, love, forgiveness, and patience.

Waiting on seeing the Lord fulfill His promises to me has been a journey. God has told me to be patient while He works all things out for my good and His glory. Because my confidence is in Christ alone, I know I will not be shaken. My emotions do not have to falter since my hope is in Christ Who is forever constant.

God wants my obedience rather than my perfection. He created me with an unusual desire to see and clean things, but I cannot let that desire distract me from seeking God first.

I have to do heart work before art work and focus on ministry before thinking about money.

My sweet children at church have my heart. They reflect our Father in vibrant ways, and it is one of my deepest joys to plant seeds in their lives!

God has blessed me in ways I have not deserved this year. His mercy and grace overwhelm me. Jesus, more than anyone else, sees the best and worse in me. Yet, He loves me more than anyone else ever could.

God is the lover of my soul, and I continuously long for Him.

I pray that the Lord will use all the pieces of my life to further His kingdom for eternity.

God is more than my faithful Father. He is my best friend.

Today I embark on chapter seventeen of my life. It is honestly crazy to think I am already this old! I am blessed beyond my wildest dreams and am overflowing with thankfulness for all God has given to me! My life is not my own. This World is not my home. I pray I spend each minute of my life intentionally making the most of every opportunity for Christ.

I sincerely strive to be an encouragement to you wherever you may be. It is probably not your birthday today, but that doesn't mean you can't start over and begin a new chapter of your life as well. Each breath we breathe is another opportunity we have to communicate with God. No matter how old you are, your life has divine purpose and potential to change the World! Never underestimate the Power living inside of you. Your life matters. You are deeply loved and already chosen. Nothing you have ever done or will ever do (no matter how bad it may be) can change God's love for you. He gave His life so that you could find yours in Him. It is okay to not know all the answers or Bible stories. God doesn't want perfection. He wants our hearts to be wholly surrendered to Him.

My birthday wish is that your spirit would be convicted, challenged, comforted, and cherished deeply today.

I am thankful for each of you!

Haley

PLANTED IN FAITH

FEBRUARY 13, 2018

Elisabeth Elliot once said, **"Don't dig up in doubt what you planted in faith."**

Yesterday, those words convicted me as I saw them posted on my sister's Instagram story.

I have been resting in holy confidence that God will have His perfect timing with a desire of my heart. Recently, the enemy has tried to use other people or things to discourage me from believing my desire will come to fruition. I have been tempted to dig up in doubt what I had planted in faith.

What have you planted in faith? Is it a relationship, dream, hope, plan, desire, hobby, or job?

Philippians 1:6 (NIV) brings me so much joy. It says, "being confident of this, that he who began a good work in you will carry it on to completion until the day of Christ Jesus."

Nothing in all of creation can stop or stand in the way of the plans God has for our lives.

God is King. He is our Father. He wants what is best for us. He isn't going to let His righteous children be shaken. He gives us mercy and grace daily. Jesus knows us better than we know ourselves. He opens up and closes doors for us, and He has already walked where we are heading.

Waiting on God's timing and continuing to have faith is not popular, but it is powerful and most rewarding.

I want to share two important quotes with you!

1. "God leaves His best for those who leave the choice with Him." -Mary Kate Robertson

2. "Those who leave everything in God's hand will eventually see God's hand in everything." -Author Unknown

Whenever we are watering seeds and waiting to see beautiful blooms, we must continue to water the seeds with patience knowing that beauty is about to be visible.

Instead of experiencing seasons of waiting, we are experiencing seasons of preparation.

THE DELIGHT MOVEMENT 2018

FEBRUARY 22, 2018

The Delight Movement has been on the forefront of my mind since this past fall. It was birthed into my spirit at the United Conference this past summer whenever Pastor Daniel Gray prophesied over me. Pastor Daniel was a guest speaker and did not know me, but he knew the God Who knows everything about me!

God told me He was going to use my words in an even greater way than He currently was.

I knew God had called me to plan a night of Godly community for middle and high school girls. As I was praying for specifics and direction, God brought the word delight to my attention at least once a day. Psalm 37:4 (NIV) became my theme verse. It says, "Take delight in the Lord, and he will give you the desires of your heart."

I wanted to encourage girls to delight in God before they desired anyone or anything else.

Around November, I sat down with a chocolate fudge sundae in my hand and began dreaming up what God had in store for the vision He gave me. I knew I needed a few months to plan The Delight Movement. Therefore, I waited until the new year to really start advertising it.

God blessed my efforts in bigger ways than I could have even imagined! A video I posted on Facebook received over three thousand views, over twenty people volunteered to help, and about sixty girls planned to attend The Delight Movement!

As God was working behind the scenes so powerfully, the enemy was too. In January, my siblings and I were in a car accident on the way to school. I was driving my car (Valerie) whenever I saw headlights coming directly towards me! I veered as far right on the road as I could to avoid a ditch full of water and a head-on collision.

On the way home from school the day of our accident, God showed me a rainbow! He had thwarted the plans of harm set out against me and my siblings. He reminded me and my loved ones that life on Earth is temporary. He challenged us to live for what truly matters for eternity.

The Sunday after the car accident, a sweet man from my church, Mr. Bobby, was used by God to invest into the ministry of The Delight Movement. His generosity and kind spirit touched me deeply. God used Mr. Bobby to remind me of His goodness!

Each time the enemy tried to bring discouragement, God brought extra encouragement!

On February 5th, Mrs. Elkie Brabble had my mom and I on her talk show named Yahweh Christian Broadcast! Being able to share such an incredible opportunity with my mom is something I'll always treasure. My mom briefly shared her testimony along with parenting tips while I talked about The Delight Movement.

The Delight Movement was held this past Saturday, February 17, 2018, at my church's chapel! We had around 85 people attend, sixty of those people being teenage girls. We were all together for four hours.

God actually changed up my schedule! He knew how everything needed to go in order for certain people to hear certain things! Also, many girls told me how God had miraculously worked it out for them to come to TDM!

While my sister Darby and I are both passionate about ministry, our personalities are completely different. God gave her musical abilities while He gave me a love for words. He knew we did not need to be the same. Rather, we needed to be different in order to complement each other best. I was so humbled and proud of my little sister for leading other girls closer to God's heart through her love of music.

Countless people were praying and fasting for The Delight Movement! We were passionately praying chains would be broken, souls would be saved, lives would be rededicated to God, seeds would be planted, and God alone would be magnified and glorified!

At the end of The Delight Movement, we asked girls to write down what God had done in their lives. Reading through those sticky notes was beyond rewarding and humbling!

I am so excited to tell you that at least three girls received salvation, at least three girls rededicated their lives to Christ, countless chains were broken, and many seeds were planted!

At The Delight Movement, girls experienced a true encounter with God! We all were ministered unto and blessed by being in God's Presence together! I am amazed at how God turned my "weakness" into my most powerful gift and weapon. In ninth grade, I had one procedure and two surgeries in my mouth. I was battling anxiety and feared public speaking, even though I knew God was calling me to it. In the past two years, God has healed my mouth and given me a spirit of freedom rather than fear. It is my desire to see my sisters in Christ and sisters who are not yet found in Christ fall madly in love with their Creator.

In my first sermon, I reminded the girls that they are **chosen, beautiful, and loved.** During our second session together, I was able to share how we, believers, can live victoriously by being intentional daily.

The Delight Movement was not about me in any way. It wasn't about Darby. It wasn't about the food, games, or giveaways either. It was solely about God our Father and Him accomplishing His purpose.

"'For my thoughts are not your thoughts, neither are your ways my ways,' declares the Lord. 'As the heavens are higher than the earth, so are my ways higher than your ways and my thoughts than your thoughts." -Isaiah 55:8-9 (NIV)

God outdid Himself at The Delight Movement to say the least! I am still so in awe that He, the God Who used Billy Graham and countless others, is the same God Who chooses to use me! He wants to use all of us, but not all of us are committed to the cause of Christ.

People with a platform are no greater than those who serve and love on the sidelines.

God has a unique and special purpose for all those who call on Him. Have *you* called on Him?

It is in the moments of "ordinary" that God prepares us for moments of extraordinary.

Never run away from or ignore the stirrings of the Holy Spirit. As Pastor Ben Prescott said at the Forward Conference, "The calling God has on your life does not just affect you. The calling on your life is strong enough to touch millions of lives and change the World!"

If Billy Graham had run away from or ignored the stirring of the Holy Spirit in his life, millions of souls would not be in Heaven today.

I am so humbled to know God chose me and gave me specific gifts to help others find true life in Him. I did not accomplish The Delight Movement by myself. My parents, siblings, teachers, family, and church body invested into this ministry.

We cannot even describe the joy we are filled with knowing God broke chains and brought His daughters back to Himself. There was not a heart untouched by the Holy Spirit Saturday night. God is continuing to work and I cannot wait to see how He forever uses The Delight Movement to change this World for Him!

With a heart full of love and thankfulness,

Haley

FIVE TRUTHS I WAS REMINDED OF WHILE BEING WITHOUT MY CAR

MARCH 5, 2018

Today I got my car back from a collision repair shop. It was gone for an exact month due to an accident in January.

God used a month without my car to remind me of a few truths!

1. To cling only to Him

My sweet friend Natalie Dodd, who is a freshmen in college this year, described her journey of comfort with me this fall. She is miles away from home without any of her family members. She is at Liberty University chasing after God's heart most passionately and clinging onto Him as her Power Source! While I was at CFAW (College for a Weekend) in September, I struggled thinking about leaving my family for college. I, personally, am extremely close to my family and love the place I get to call home. Natalie reminded me that leaving home for college is one of the first steps of growing up. **College is a time when you leave comfort for the call of Christ.** I am no longer worried about leaving home. God has been teaching me that He alone is where my identity and comfort can be found. I am not going to find true joy in my family, friends, home, church, grades, pictures, blog posts, abilities, or appearance. A prom date or boyfriend will not fill my cup up with God's unwavering peace either.

While all of those things can be used for good and even Godly purposes, they cannot fill my longing for God Himself.

2. Beautiful things do not happen over night

An abundant, pure, passionate, contagious, and consistent relationship with Jesus Christ takes time to grow. We must not expect to be intimate with God if we are not in His Presence. *We have to start seeking God where we are at with what we have. If we wait to seek Him "when we are ready", we will never seek Him.* Instead of writing down good intentions, let's start putting action behind our convictions.

3. I am not going to get more of God if I am seeking lesser things

Sunday I ate cake for breakfast and ice cream for supper! I realize that wasn't healthy, but I enjoyed the sweets whenever I ate them. As a result of filling myself up with sugar, I was extremely tired. Do you think I expected to be filled with energy knowing the effects of what I had consumed? No, I knew my choices were not the best for my health; but they would give me temporary pleasure. This thought applies to our spiritual lives. **Whatever we fill ourselves up with will be what we overflow with. We cannot give in to temporary pleasures and expect to receive eternal blessings.**

4. God does not do anything by accident

Although our prayers may not come to fruition in the ways we had planned, they will be answered in the best ways possible. God created time. He created you and I. He holds the entire World inside of His hands. He already has each page of our lives written inside of a book.

"Your eyes saw my unformed body; all the days ordained for me were written in your book before one of them came to be." -Psalm 139:16 (NIV)

We do not have to be disappointed whenever we hear unexpected things. God is our Hope and Power Source. He is in control. He only has His absolute best for our lives. **Nothing can stop or stand in the way of the plans He has for us.**

5. I cannot control the enemy's attacks, but I can control how I react to them

My parents and I were originally told my car would be fixed in less than two weeks. When the day came for Valerie (my car) to be picked up, we received a phone call from the collision shop with disappointing news. They had broken a glass while trying to replace it. This process was repeated at least three times. We would look forward to getting my car only to be told another glass was broken. I did not always react to those disappointing phone calls with a good attitude. I was honestly upset and wanted to leave a bad review on the company's website! *God pricked my heart as He asked me if my attitude towards those people working on my car was bringing Him more glory.*

We never know who is watching the way we act and react to the enemy's attacks.

Whenever we face a hard situation, we are also blessed with a huge opportunity to illuminate the darkness with light.

"The light shines in the darkness, and the darkness has not overcome it." - John 1:5 (NIV)

"And we know that in all things God works for the good of those who love him, who have been called according to his purpose." -Romans 8:28 (NIV)

As Caleb Stanley recently said, "keep stepping." God hasn't brought you this far to abandon you or stop using your life to touch others! The things ahead of you are greater than anything you have left behind. Don't look back or turn back to your old ways. If the enemy is working against you, know God is working through you! You are victorious through Jesus Christ. Walk in courage. Continue to keep putting your best foot forward.

I am here for you and love you!

Haley

NEW BEGINNINGS

APRIL 3, 2018

Beauty is everywhere.

I have just emerged from a season of struggling. Struggling to hear God's voice most clearly. Struggling with changes on the horizon. Struggling to trust God's purpose even when it didn't look like what I had planned.

God has been beyond good to me! I am overflowing with gratitude today for Who He is and everything He has done.

During The Victor, a ministry of my church, God used an encounter with a humble man to challenge me. I was in the balcony whenever I extended a bright prayer card to a man I did not know. He was accepting of the prayer card. Seconds after he received it, he asked for help. He could not write on his own. I gently bent down to where the man was sitting and asked what his need was. He desperately wanted to see his sister find new life in Christ. He was not ashamed of his inability to write. He boldly admitted his weakness in order to receive God's supernatural strength.

I needed to be more like this man.

I had been struggling with my own weaknesses. Struggling to trust in God's purpose despite my failed plans.

Walking around the parking lot of my church with a runny nose and a hungry heart, God bent down to hear my requests. He didn't laugh at me for being human and weak. He was drawn to my weak areas because they are the areas He died for. Jesus doesn't expect us to be perfect, my friend. He wants us to come to Him humbly as we are. *He will meet us where we are at and take us where we need to go.*

We cannot give up whenever we struggle to see beauty, hope, or answered prayers. **God does the most crucial work in our lives whenever we are vulnerable.** The soil of our hearts must be worked with. Weeds must be pulled up. Vitamins have to be deposited.

Jesus is the Gardener of our souls.

He brings beauty out of the darkness. **He plants seeds before we see fruit.**

Do not be ashamed of your weaknesses, inabilities, or shortcomings. **God is able to deposit more of Himself into us whenever we are empty.**

God's perfect purposes are far greater than our best plans.

With my prom date situation, I have seen this to be true. I know God was really waiting for the posture of my heart to change before He revealed His plans to me. He was waiting for me to desire Him first. He wanted me to truly believe that Christ alone was more than enough for me.

This world is full of false hope, brother or sister. While it is so easy to become distracted from your true Purpose, there is such a great need for your life! You are living and breathing for a Purpose extraordinarily bigger than yourself. God is going to use your life to impact millions of people. I truly believe that with my whole heart. Do not give in to Satan's lies. **Do not trade God's best for what is familiar.** Our calling is not one of comfort. Rather, it is one of growth.

How is God bringing beauty out of the darkness in your life? How is God stretching you in order for you to grow?

"The grass withers, the flowers fade, but the word of our God remains forever." -Isaiah 40:8 (CSB)

Our God is all powerful. He is bigger than any mountain we will ever face.

I pray we will develop greater faith, vibrant love, and endless passion this spring!

God is for us, my friend! With Him, we will never be shaken. Stand tall. Keep stepping. Be cleansed by God's grace and forgiveness. Continue to make the enemy mad. You mean more to me than you even know. Thank you for running this race with me!

Full of true Hope,

Haley

THE WAY THAT YOU ARE LIVING MATTERS

MAY 26, 2018

God prodded my heart in Arby's yesterday afternoon.

The young woman who stood behind the cash register had a life I knew pretty much nothing about.

God wanted me to be meaningful with my encounter with her.

As she swept the floor and cleaned up the restaurant, she needed to know she was loved and appreciated. The work she was doing mattered. She may have been overlooked at home or school, but God knew her by name!

Walking beside her as she was cleaning, I simply, but intentionally said, *"Thank you for all you do!"*

I questioned if I was supposed to say more, but my short sentence had a powerful impact on the girl. I could tell she was not used to hearing comments of appreciation.

Her response to me was *"Thank you for being so nice!"*

—

God didn't overlook the young woman working at Arby's and He does not overlook you. He sees you exactly where you are at. The way that you are currently living your life matters.

If Jesus is breathing inside of you, you have such power and authority through Him! Satan trembles as you keep taking steps towards God and in ministry.

The way that you are living matters. God sees you. His eye is on you. You matter to Him. Your life has eternal value and worth!

Jesus longs for you. He wants you to be close to Him.

God sees you as you doodle in class.

He knows your thoughts at ball practice.

He holds your heart and all that it longs for.

Jesus is reminding you that the work you are doing is important.

The long days and short nights do not go unnoticed.

Both followers of Jesus and lost people look to you. You give them Hope of Something (Someone) greater. You bring joy, peace, purity, and laughter to a conversation. Your peers honor and respect you for your faith. Whether they admit it or not, you are leaving God's fingerprints on their hearts. God is using you to reach them for Him.

Do not let Satan steal what God has given you. Do not be distracted by unfulfilled longings or requests. Keep your eyes on Jesus. He is the Author and Perfecter of our faith.

Do not tremble in fear. March on boldly.

Walk into new places and watch God's plan unfold.

You are a light of God. You reflect Him. **You are not here for yourself.**

Who has God placed in your life to touch for Him?

I believe Jesus would be accepted more often if we chose to share His love in tangible ways each day of our lives.

"Therefore, since we are surrounded by such a huge crowd of witnesses to the life of faith, let us strip off every weight that slows us down, especially the sin that so easily trips us up. And let us run with endurance the race God has set before us. We do this by keeping our eyes on Jesus, the champion who initiates

and perfects our faith. Because of the joy awaiting him, he endured the cross, disregarding its shame. Now he is seated in the place of honor beside God's throne. Think of all the hostility he endured from sinful people; then you won't become weary and give up." -Hebrews 12:1-3 (NLT)

THE DRY SEASON IS OVER

JUNE 30, 2018

God has shown me so many truths this past month. It has been a month of fully consecrating myself to the Lord while also feeling very distant from Him. My quiet time has become loud as God has opened my eyes to see His Word for what it truly is-*alive*.

In a season of new beginnings and a lot of endings, **Jesus told me to stop worrying about my life.** I often found myself being asked about my plans for the future and always responding in a tone of doubt. I truly desire to go to Liberty University after I graduate high school next spring. Being aware of the high cost of attending my dream school, my response to people would always contain "if I get the scholarships."

My Heavenly Father convicted me to stop doubting who He is and what He is capable of doing for me.

Instead of asking Jesus to provide the scholarships I need, I am now thanking Him for the ones He has already provided.

Faith is believing in what we cannot yet see. Faith goes beyond our focus and is reached in God's view.

Whenever I read Hebrews 11, which is known as the chapter of faith in the Bible, God showed me so much! I challenge you to read it as well. In chapter 11, the Bible mentions Biblical leaders who had extraordinary faith! Having faith was not the only thing each of these people had in common.

-God made the impossible possible in their lives

-They trusted God to do what He said He would do

-God exceeded their expectations

-They were willing to give up what they loved most because they loved God more

God is faithful! Let me also remind you that **Noah built the ark before he saw the flood.** That statement from the Lord blows me away! Noah believed that God would do what He told him. Noah didn't doubt the Lord. He simply obeyed, even if he was the only one.

"By faith Noah, after he was warned about what was not yet seen and motivated by godly fear, built an ark to deliver his family. By faith he condemned the world and became an heir of the righteousness that comes by faith." - Hebrews 11:7 (CSB)

In a season of many unknowns and changes, I rest in the fact that my God is good. *His goodness does not change based upon my circumstances.* **"Jesus Christ is the same yesterday, today, and forever."** -Hebrews 13:8 (CSB)

While I was at Liberty University last week, I became overwhelmed by my decided major. I had my degree plan memorized and had already been quoting it ("Elementary Education in the area of English and minor in Women's Leadership").

God is taking control and letting me enjoy sitting in the passenger seat.

My plans are changing and that's okay as long as Jesus is the One Who is changing them.

Two days in a row, He comforted me with the Bible verses listed below:

***"I will instruct you and teach you in the way you should go; I will counsel you with my loving eye on you."* -Psalm 32:8 (NIV)**

"You make known to me the path of life; you will fill me with joy in your presence, with eternal pleasures at your right hand." -Psalm 16:11 (NIV)

I am now praying about majoring in Christian Leadership and Church Ministries while having a focus in Women's Leadership. *My God is not going to lead me to do something I won't enjoy.* As Psalm 16:11 says, God is going to fill us with joy in His presence. **His Presence will always be with His will.**

I am realizing that I am not in control and that God is! He knows what is best for me and is going to get me where He wants me to be! I do not have to worry about anything as long as I am with Him.

Satan loves to feed our minds with lies. He wants us to believe God is distant from us and that we are distant from God. That is quite a lie, my friend! Our God is close, and He is near! Jesus gave His everything and died on the cross so that we could know Him intimately! Jesus raised Himself from the grave so we could be watered by Him daily. **Jesus is real, and He is alive!** We must stop believing lies from the enemy!

I want the P's of God rather than the D's of Satan. God provides peace, passion, purpose, protection, and purity while Satan offers discouragement, destruction, death, and devastation.

We must stop believing Satan's lies! We are not far from God's love. While nothing in all of Creation can separate us from the love of God, our sin prevents us from having intimacy with Him. Don't let sin keep you from our Heavenly Father, brother or sister! Jesus, as any good parent, longs for His children to be close to Him. He does not want us to be far away. **Jesus' blood will cover our sins the moment we ask for forgiveness.**

One of my favorite personal stories was written by Bob Goff in his book *Love Does*. While driving his jeep home from church, an eighty-seven year old lady ran into him with her car. Bob, thankfully, was okay, but his jeep was ruined. Bob assured Lynn, the lady who hit him, that everything was fine. She kept apologizing and even calling Bob expressing her grief over what had happened. In order to quit receiving these calls from Lynn whom he had already forgiven, Bob sent her a bouquet of flowers with a note that read, "Dear Lynn, it was great running into you… Now stop calling me! Bob." In the words of the author, "I think Lynn got the message. I was fine, and I wanted her to be fine too. I wanted her to forgive herself, to realize we all make mistakes. I'm glad I ran into Lynn, and I'm glad she kept calling too. It taught me something about faith. It taught me that when God is big enough and loves me enough to say He forgives me, I should actually believe Him. I mean, I shouldn't keep feeling bad about all of the times I've messed up because that's ignoring what God said, just like Lynn ignored what I said. When I don't trust God's forgiveness, it's kind of like saying I really don't believe He's that good. Lynn made me think I should stop asking God to forgive me over and over when He's made it clear He already has."

I love this analogy of God's forgiveness. If we ask God to forgive us from something, He will forgive us!

"For I am convinced that neither death nor life, neither angels nor demons, neither the present nor the future, nor any powers, neither height nor depth, nor anything else in all creation, will be able to separate us from the love of God that is in Christ Jesus our Lord." -Romans 8:38-39 (NIV)

While platforms and fame can seem appealing to us, let's remind ourselves that it's not about us. I never want to be like Lucifer who thought he knew it all. Our little minds are like ants compared to our Father's wisdom! Let's stay humble.

God is giving us new beginnings. He is doing so much behind the scenes for us! He fights for us daily.

I love picturing Jesus as the Gardener of our souls. He handles us with such tenderness and care. He knows when the soil of our hearts is dry. He always knows exactly what we need. As said in the song There Is A Cloud by Elevation Worship, "The dry season is over."

I love you guys and am so thankful for our Father's love! What has God been doing in your life? I would love to hear and be encouraged by your testaments!

With love,

Haley

TRUSTING GOD IN THE UNSEEN

AUGUST 1, 2018

God is a God of peace. Disorder, chaos, fear, and anxiety have no place in our Father. Sitting on the beach, a place of peace, I found myself full of anxiety about the upcoming school year. It hasn't even started yet.

The enemy has been attacking my thoughts, and I have not been too positive about starting school. In June, I said goodbye to the school I have been at my whole life. I have always loved that school and still do. It wasn't until the last few months of my junior year that God opened my heart to embracing a new season. I knew my brother and sister would be changing schools, and I couldn't imagine doing my senior year without them. Jesus used the first chapter of Deuteronomy to give me confirmation about leaving Bethel. On the sides of the pages in my Bible, I wrote the things listed below:

- It is time for a change
- Keep stepping
- Walk into and through the doors God has opened for you
- Stop trying to be and do what only God can be and do
- Take possession of what God has given you
- Don't be afraid or discouraged
- The land God is giving you is good
- Be willing to go where God is leading you
- Don't give in to the voices of discouragement
- God goes before you and fights for you
- Remember how God has carried you this far

"And you saw in the wilderness how the Lord your God carried you as a man carries his son all along the way you traveled until you reached this place."
-Deuteronomy 1:31 (CSB)

-God has been making a way and preparing you and many others for this journey

What new adventure has God set before you? Are you welcoming this new season or are you, like me, struggling to find clarity? Don't get me wrong. I know God has called me to this new place, and I couldn't imagine myself doing senior year anywhere else. I am thankful for this new season. It is a stepping stone of transition. God is doing bigger things than I can even imagine. In *The Circle Maker*, Mark Batterson wrote, "Take a step of faith when God gives you a vision because you trust that the One Who gave you a vision is going to make provision. And for the record, if the vision is from God, it will most definitely be beyond your means."

Wow. God gives us visions beyond our means so that He can receive the glory from our stories. As most of you know, I desire to attend Liberty University. It is my dream school. On July 18, 2018 I experienced God's faithfulness like never before. One little navy blue box meant much more to me than the college acceptance letter itself. My acceptance to Liberty had God's fingerprints stamped all over it. Standing in my bedroom, I was reminded of the journey God has carried me through thus far. He has never left my side. He has always been faithful. I have really been thinking a lot about God's faithfulness here lately. Our Father never changes. He is absolutely perfect. God doesn't have to have us, but He chooses to love on us daily. His love is true. It is the only thing that can satisfy my soul.

As I savor the last days of summer, I don't want to doubt what my God can do for me. His love is so forceful! God's creation really points back to Him. It is beautiful and full of peace. As God's creation, we also reflect our Daddy.

I want to be salt and light. In the CSB version of the Bible, Matthew 5:13-16 states, "You are the salt of the earth. But if the salt should lose its taste, how can it be made salty? It's no longer good for anything but to be thrown out and trampled under people's feet. You are the light of the world. A city situated on a hill cannot be hidden. No one lights a lamp and puts it under a basket, but rather on a lampstand, and it gives light for all who are in the house. In the same way, let your light shine before others, so that they may see your good works and give glory to your Father in heaven."

Our lives are not about us. Like light, I want to let people know someone else has been where they are at. They are not alone. There is always something more with God where you are at. The Light drives out all fear. Like the ocean, I long to leave a residue of Jesus on people. At the touch of salt, wounds may sting, but they will eventually heal. The salt reaches people the ocean will never see. I pray that we, as God's children, carry God's Presence with us in such a contagious and real way.

Let's not worry about our lives. Matthew 6:25-34 (CSB) states, "'Therefore I tell you: Don't worry about your life, what you will eat or what you will drink; or about your body, what you will wear. Isn't life more than food and the body more than clothing? Consider the birds of the sky: They don't sow or reap or gather into barns, yet your heavenly Father feeds them. Aren't you worth more than they? Can any of you add one moment to his life-span by worrying? And why do you worry about clothes? Observe how the wildflowers of the field grow: They don't labor or spin thread. Yet I tell you that not even Solomon in all his splendor was adorned like one of these. If that's how God clothes the grass of the field, which is here today and thrown into the furnace tomorrow, won't he do much more for you—you of little faith? So don't worry, saying, 'What will we eat?' or 'What will we drink?' or 'What will we wear?' For the Gentiles eagerly seek all these things, and your heavenly Father knows that you need them. But seek first the kingdom of God and his righteousness, and all these things will be provided for you. Therefore don't worry about tomorrow, because tomorrow will worry about itself. Each day has enough trouble of its own."

This message really stood out to me whenever Shiloh Collect sent me a print containing the words "do not worry about your life." In the midst of applying to scholarships, starting my senior year, and striving to have strong faith, God speaks these words into my sprit. Perhaps you need to be reminded of them too. Your circumstances are not bigger than your God. Our Father controls the waves. He controls everything. We aren't the ones in control. Only God can make the impossible things possible in our lives. "For nothing will be impossible with God." -Luke 1:37 (CSB)

Never stop seeking our Father's heart, my friend. There is more in store than what we can see. Our Jesus carries us on His shoulders. He holds our burdens, desires, and cares inside of His strong hands. Let's rest inside of His freedom. We can't let Satan attack what God is going to use most. We have victory and peace because of Who our Daddy is!

I love you guys and am so grateful for you.

Haley

REVISITING THE CAVE

AUGUST 13, 2018

The kings of fear inside of my mind have been jostling around.

My Bible Study group discussed Joshua 10:16-27 last Tuesday. There is a message in it that I want to share with you. Let's first read the passage of Scripture together to better understand the lesson.

"Now the five defeated kings had fled and hidden in the cave at Makkedah. It was reported to Joshua: 'The five kings have been found; they are hiding in the cave at Makkedah.' Joshua said, 'Roll large stones against the mouth of the cave, and station men by it to guard the kings. But as for the rest of you, don't stay there. Pursue your enemies and attack them from behind. Don't let them enter their cities, for the Lord your God has handed them over to you.' So Joshua and the Israelites finished inflicting a terrible slaughter on them until they were destroyed, although a few survivors ran away to the fortified cities. The people returned safely to Joshua in the camp at Makkedah. And no one dared to threaten the Israelites. Then Joshua said, 'Open the mouth of the cave, and bring those five kings to me out of there.' That is what they did. They brought the five kings of Jerusalem, Hebron, Jarmuth, Lachish, and Eglon to Joshua out of the cave. When they had brought the kings to him, Joshua summoned all the men of Israel and said to the military commanders who had accompanied him, 'Come here and put your feet on the necks of these kings.' So the commanders came forward and put their feet on their necks. Joshua said to them, 'Do not be afraid or discouraged. Be strong and courageous, for the Lord will do this to all the

enemies you fight.' After this, Joshua struck them down and executed them. He hung their bodies on five trees and they were there until evening. At sunset Joshua commanded that they be taken down from the trees and thrown into the cave where they had hidden. Then large stones were placed against the mouth of the cave, and the stones are still there today." -Joshua 10:16-27 (CSB)

We all have caves in our lives. They are tucked away so that most people cannot see them. What is hiding inside of your cave? Is it fear, insecurity, rejection, anxiety, shame, or past regrets?

The things hiding inside the caves of our lives are full of destruction. The five kings Joshua faced were out to harm him. Nothing inside of a hidden cave is going to better us. Satan uses the caves of our minds and the caves of our pasts as objects of ruin. I believe Satan longs to trap you and I inside a box of limitations. Our enemy wants to steal our joy, zeal, passion, excitement, and freedom. Yes, freedom. Satan is really after our freedom. He wants us to be held captive by someone or something so that we will not be effective in God's kingdom. For a long season, Satan used fear to entrap me. It made me weak. Fear wrung life and joy out from me. The battle I faced was held in my mind, but it affected every other aspect of my life.

For the past two days, I have heard the kings of fear speaking lies in my mind. They have been spitting anxiety out over me regarding my new school year. Satan wants to scare me by giving me thoughts about the past. As I heard the kings inside of my mind moving around, my Heavenly Father, the One true King, helped me remember the lesson I first encountered in Sadie Robertson's Bible study resource titled *Awaken*.

It is time for us to revisit the cave. Revisiting something can sometimes be scary, but our God has not given us a spirit of fear. In the King James Version, 2

Timothy 1:7 says, "For God hath not given us the spirit of fear; but of power, and of love, and of a sound mind." I challenge you to write that verse down and hide it in your heart. Fear is not from God. Shame is not from God. Anxiety is not from God. Pain is not from God. Insecurity is not from God either. Jesus Christ died on the cross and gave Himself up for us so that we can be children of God. Being a child of God changes everything, my friend. Because we are children of the Most High God, we are not held captive by the things of this world. Satan has no grip on us. Sin has been paid for by Jesus. Death has lost its sting.

What kings are moving around in your mind and life today? In what ways is the enemy trying to enslave you?

On the morning I was set free from fear, the lady praying with me said that our God is bigger than the things we face! There is nothing bigger than our God. I have not forgotten those words of truth spoken to me.

We must kill the things lingering around in the caves of our minds and lives. We cannot leave anything alive in there. We must go revisit the cave. We have to get rid of the things being used by Satan to kill us! I love how Sadie Robertson said, "The enemy attacked me right where the Lord was going to call me in speaking and writing. He was trying to shut up my voice for the Lord." That could not be more true for you and me too. **The enemy always attacks the people, places, and things God is going to use most!**

Are you ready to go break some necks? That sounds terrible, but it is necessary in defeating Satan. Let's defeat fear today. Let's defeat insecurity, shame, and past regrets right now. Defeat anything that is holding you back from being who God created you to be! Let's empty out our caves today and close them back up clean so that nothing else can enter into them.

I want us to live in freedom this school year and forever. I never want us to be held captive by lies from Satan. We have to fill ourselves up with Truth and ask God to guard our minds. Fall into Him today, brother or sister. Jesus never looks at you with disgust. Yes, He hates your sin, but He loves you. That is why He gave up everything to forgive you. He will make you clean. He longs to give you a fresh start. Claim and receive it today.

Striving to live in freedom always,

Haley

THRIVING THROUGH TRANSITIONS

SEPTEMBER 2, 2018

Our changing schools situation has been the craziest thing. At the end of last year, I wasn't ready for junior year to end. I knew leaving Bethel was God's plan, but I was emotional about it. Over the summer, I was really struggling to be positive about starting my senior year. I wasn't upset about changing schools. Rather, I was clinging onto my familiar schedule. Up until the day before school began, I stayed clenched onto summer. The night before school started, my class had a senior meeting at Starbucks. I was thankful God allowed me to meet most of my classmates before the first day of school! I also had to kill the kings of fear lingering around in my mind before starting a new chapter.

August 15, 2018 was a day I hope I'll never forget! It was a day filled with God's guidance, courage, boldness, and Presence! I walked the halls of a school that once felt like uncharted territory to me. Here I am now a few weeks later. My school feels like a home God has given to me for this season. I don't feel like I am shadowing a class. *Instead, I realize I play a vital role in my classmates' lives!* In the short time I have been at my new school, I've matured so much. *I'm learning how to better share and defend what I believe without turning away people with different views.* **I have gone from being ready to finish high school to not really wanting it to end.** I am enjoying school and finding many reasons to laugh each day.

I never would have thought that this transition could be *so* good. Once again, I knew it was God's plan, but I had to trust Him with the details. I went from feeling in control to learning new ropes. *God has been teaching me that unfamiliarity isn't something to run from. It is actually something to run to if God has placed it in our paths.*

While getting to know new people and forming new friendships, God has reminded me that only **He is my joyometer**. My joy isn't dependent upon my interactions with other people. **No friendship can take the place of God's friendship in my life.** While this is true, I have also been relying on God to give me balance in growing in these new friendships.

There are so many needs before me and you each day! Although I have had trouble opening my own locker (and even forgetting the right code), God has allowed me to help someone else open their locker. There are other new students at my school who are new to our country! **When we take our eyes off of ourselves, God will show us Himself through countless other people!**

God has placed us where we are at now because that is where He needs us most! That quote from Pastor Mitch Sugg constantly runs through my mind! If my family had not of been obedient to God and embraced a season of change, we would have missed out on so many opportunities God had for us! I encourage you to embrace whatever season you are in. One of my teachers, Mr. Paul, said a quote the other day that has really stuck with me. He said, **"If you are living to please God, you can do kingdom work wherever you go."** Our Father is going to make sure we get to the places He has in store for us.

Because I have been spending a lot of time talking to a new friend at school, that person is most included in the stories I share with my loved ones in the afternoons. The Holy Spirit told me that this is my answer to talking about Jesus more in my everyday conversations. **We are going to talk about who we spend the most time with.** Are we seeking Jesus so much each day that He oozes out of us? **Our time with God is more valuable than our time with**

anyone else. *We don't just get to go to church once a week. We get to live in God every day!*

I challenge us to not just sit in a room with Jesus. Let's look at Him face to face, share our hearts, and be intentional with our encounters with Him. We serve a God Who doesn't leave us wondering how He feels about us. Jesus has made and continues to make His love for us known. He continues to pursue us even when we don't realize it. He is always the answer to what our souls long for.

I pray that Jesus is our Core. He is our source for everything that we need. With Him, we lack no good thing. Psalm 34:9-10 (NIV) says, "Fear the Lord, you his holy people, for those who fear him lack nothing. The lions may grow weak and hungry, but those who seek the Lord lack no good thing."

Luke 6:45 (NIV) states, "A good man brings good things out of the good stored up in his heart, and an evil man brings evil things out of the evil stored up in his heart. For the mouth speaks what the heart is full of."

I want the overflow of our hearts to reflect Jesus because we have filled ourselves up with Him alone.

Keep living with Purpose, my friend! I would love to hear what God has been teaching you!

Sincerely,

Haley Wade

IMMEASURABLY MORE

OCTOBER 1, 2018

The season of life I am currently in is sweet. It is full of the most unexpected blessings, the faithfulness of God, and tough questions. I am constantly bringing my messy heart before God and asking Him to make me clean. Here lately, I have been seeking Jesus for purity and holiness. I am asking Him to guard my heart and guide my steps. God's plans for us are good. They are never to harm us. Rather, they are to give us hope and a future (Jeremiah 29:11). We can do all things because He is the One Who gives us strength (Philippians 4:13). We are not going to grow tired or weary in doing good. We are going to reap a harvest at the proper time if we do not give up (Galatians 6:9).

Never forget that God hears your prayers! Recently, our Father astounded me by revealing how involved He is in the details of my life. Jesus doesn't miss a thing, my friend! He is listening to our conversations and pays attention to the desires of our hearts.

Jesus has also been reminding me that things full of comfort aren't necessarily His best. If God is leading you into a new season full of unknowns, I greatly urge you to keep following Him. Psalm 16:11(NIV) says, "You make known to me the path of life; you will fill me with joy in your presence, with eternal pleasures at your right hand."

I could never fully express how thankful I am for this new chapter of my life. I had always dreamed of graduating from the school I grew up in. As a little girl, I envisioned myself being on the homecoming court senior year. As our precious Father urged my heart to follow His lead at the end of last year, I exchanged my good for His best. Wow! I could never tell you how good our Father's plans are, brother or sister! This has been the absolute best school year of my life. It has been the most amazing and surprising experience. During the summer, I was truly focused on Liberty and graduating from high school. To be honest with you, I wasn't planning on forming heartfelt connections my senior year. God has really blown me away! He has woven together the most beautiful story to give Him the most glory.

There are a few little lessons of great impact that I want to share with you.

1. Permissible vs. Beneficial

This lesson took a while for me to learn. Jesus actually revealed the thought to me through multiple books and magazines.

1 Corinthians 10:23 (CSB) says, "'Everything is permissible,' but not everything is beneficial. 'Everything is permissible,' but not everything builds up."

Permissible things are okay. They aren't necessarily bad. In fact, permissible things are allowed.

Beneficial things, though, are helpful, good for us, edifying, and worth our time. People who are beneficial accomplish things far greater than themselves. I believe that all beneficial people and things have Jesus at their core. Are all of our decisions, conversations, and actions revolving around Him? Are we seeking to make God's power known?

Instead of choosing what we can get by with, Jesus has called us to fill our lives with people and things that will give Him the most glory! I long for the relationships in my life to be beneficial. I want God's best. I don't want what is easy or okay. Why settle for less when Jesus has given us the most extraordinary lives possible?

2. Immeasurably More

Ephesians 3:20 (NIV) exclaims, "Now to him who is able to do immeasurably more than all we ask or imagine, according to his power that is at work within us,"

Jesus is able to do immeasurably more than all we ask for, dream of, think of, or imagine. I don't know about you, but my dreams can get crazy at times! Yet, our Jesus is able to do far more than we can even imagine. Why do we underestimate His power so often, my friend? We trust Jesus to meet our daily needs. Why do we doubt what He can do in the desires of our hearts? **The dreams and desires placed within you are not by accident.** You never know how God is going to use your gifts and skills to bring you closer to Him, give Him more glory, and point countless people closer to His love! Never give in to the enemy's lies that whisper doubt and disbelief to you. Our God is a God of clarity. Chaos never comes from Him.

I pray that you realize there is always more of Jesus for us to discover. We could never run out of things to thank God for. How is your heart doing tonight? What do you need to lay down at Jesus' feet? It is time to stop believing Satan's lies. Claim and declare God's Truth over your heart, mind, and life.

God has been with you every step you have taken. He will never leave your side.

Cling onto our faithful Father and Friend. He isn't scared of your mess. Jesus longs to make you clean.

I am fighting for you through prayer and encouragement.

Your sister in Christ,

Haley

DOUBT DOESN'T COME FROM GOD

OCTOBER 12, 2018

The devil always targets the people, places, and things God is going to use most. I firmly believe this truth.

We usually face the most opposition whenever God is working most powerfully in our lives. There are so many things Jesus does behind the scenes of our lives daily. Is your biggest dream coming to life? What doors is God opening and closing for you? What about your new friendship that is bringing Jesus glory? Satan is ticked off because he realizes the Power that lives within you.

Instead of being filled with holy confidence, are you struggling with insecure thoughts? I have battled these struggles too, my friend.

My Abba is bringing so many of my dreams to life. He is fulfilling my hungering desires. I forever want the peace, protection, passion, purity, and provision that comes from Christ alone. He is on our side and is fighting for us always. There isn't a day that Jesus doesn't walk with us. Are we walking with Him daily?

You are leaking over, my brother or sister. Do you even realize how influential your life is? Keep your eyes on Jesus. Keep pushing through the hard days. Your faith is contagious.

God used Hebrews 12:1-2 (CSB) to fill me back up with Himself this afternoon. Let's read it together. *"Therefore, since we also have such a large cloud of witnesses surrounding us, let us lay aside every hindrance and the sin that so easily ensnares us. Let us run with endurance the race that lies before us, keeping our eyes on Jesus, the source and perfecter of our faith. For the joy that lay before him, he endured the cross, despising the shame, and sat down at the right hand of the throne of God."*

Around this verse in my Bible, I wrote little notes to explain each phrase.

-Your life doesn't just affect you. Your life is an example to the believers in speech, in conduct, in love, in faith, and in purity.

1 Timothy 4:12 (NIV) says, "Don't let anyone look down on you because you are young, but set an example for the believers in speech, in conduct, in love, in faith and in purity."

The enemy wants to get rid of you sharing the Gospel. He wants to discourage, destroy, and devastate you using doubt. Satan wants you and I to live in fear and insecurities. He doesn't want us to experience God's abundance. The devil knows you pray big prayers that point to your massive God! Your life reflects Jesus, and that ticks Satan off. With Jesus, we experience fullness and joy. We must be on guard and always prepared for the fiery darts the enemy is throwing at us. Satan has been defeated by Jesus. Therefore, we don't have to be afraid of him.

-Step out of the traps you are standing in.

-If you are going to run, run with **everything** you have.

-The race you're running isn't behind you. Your race lies before you. **Keep taking each good step God blesses you with.**

I am learning that I never have to fear an unexpected season of life. My Daddy always has a good next step for me to take. He is a God of immeasurably more. God never gives me less than His best for my life.

I am hanging onto Jesus and seeking Him for peace and discomfort in making decisions. God's peace is one of my favorite things to experience.

I have been blessed with one of the sweetest friendships of my life this school year. I'm realizing that doing life with other believers truly refines us. Although friendships and relationships can sometimes seem messy, they reveal the true parts of who we are. Is Jesus our Core? Without Him, we are like nasty bags of trash on the inside. We can try to stay perfectly wrapped on the outside, but those layers will quickly fall off.

Do you want to hear something cool? **Vulnerability leads to connectivity.** Let Jesus use this season or friendship in your life to refine you. As you experience pressures and fires you have never felt before, trust that God is shaping you into exactly who He has made you to be. Jesus rids us of ourselves so that we can be fully filled with Him.

Don't let Satan keep you from the blessings God is trying to bestow upon you.

-The Source and Perfecter of our faith is Jesus. We aren't our own sources of faith. We can't fill a source that isn't us. We must simply place ourselves under the tap of God's big well of faith. He is our Perfecter. Our load to be perfect isn't carried by us. We are not perfect, and Jesus knows that. He loves us anyway. God is the One Who perfects us and makes us complete.

"Therefore, since we also have such a large cloud of witnesses surrounding us, let us lay aside every hindrance and the sin that so easily ensnares us. Let us run with endurance the race that lies before us, keeping our

eyes on Jesus, the source and perfecter of our faith. For the joy that lay before him, he endured the cross, despising the shame, and sat down at the right hand of the throne of God." -Hebrews 12:1-2 (CSB)

-In the most excruciating pain, Jesus knew He had joy that lay before Him. In our most trying times, we must not forget the joy that lies before us.

Our conversations, motives, actions, and intentions matter. I have been deeply longing to purely reflect Jesus in all of my ways. Instead of focusing on our mistakes and inabilities, I challenge us to look to Jesus and speak Truth over our minds. We don't have time to waste. The opportunities we are given daily are valuable. Let's be intentional with our friendships, school years, family members, and church services.

Ask God to destroy the doubt in your life. Don't leave any doors cracked for the enemy to slide in. We can't be naive to the enemy's tactics. We must be aware of the constant battle that is going on for our time, attention, and affections. Our God is greater, my friend! He has defeated Satan and stands victorious forever!

ONE GOOD STEP AT A TIME

NOVEMBER 13, 2018

God is teaching me that I am not in control. Over the summer, I trusted my sweet Father with the unknowns of changing schools my senior year of high school. He gave me the best transition possible and has filled my life with the most unexpected blessings!

This post could be titled so many different things. My days have been absolutely full of common themes from the Lord.

What has God been doing in your life, my friend? As I share the work God has been doing in and through me, I pray that you are inspired to fulfill the callings He has placed within you!

I'm a planner. I love to know where I am headed next and what I need to do in order to get there. Jesus has emerged fun into my senior year in ways I haven't experienced before. I'm constantly being reminded that God's love does not limit me. Our Father's love sets us free. It gives us freedom.

As I am enjoying the unexpected blessings God has given to me, I have honestly been struggling to be excited about college next year. Now, if you had of talked to me last year, I would have told you I was ready to go to Liberty University! I was pretty ready to be done with high school and planned on meeting my future husband and best friends in college.

God continues to humble, challenge, change, and grow me each day. While at Liberty over the weekend, God used the voices of my loved ones to speak to me. Yes, I love Liberty. I love the people there. Most importantly, I love the way Jesus is present and active on Liberty's campus through His people. I've prayed about God's will for my college decisions since the eighth grade. It has been such a fun, interesting, and special journey! While I sometimes think I would like to receive the detailed plan God has for my life, I really don't. **The plans the Lord has for us are bigger and better than what we can even comprehend. Abba leads us into the plans He has for us one good step at a time. There is always a good next step with the Lord.**

As I'm applying to scholarships, my family has challenged me to pay attention to closed doors. Who likes closed doors? Do you? I honestly hadn't stopped to realize the significance of the doors I saw God closing in my life. Yes, I still desire to go to Liberty and know that God has a plan for me being there. What I am currently praying about is God's perfect timing in me getting to where He wants me to be. While walking and talking with Him this afternoon, **Jesus reminded me that He is going to get me to where He wants me to be; even if it means taking a different route than the one I originally had planned.**

Can I tell you something, my friend? I believe our Father really just wants us to surrender our plans to Him. Daddy Jesus really wants us to be willing to obey and trust Him even in unexpected and new places. God's plans for us are always better than the plans we have for ourselves. Our Father also places nudges within us that give us hints to His future plans. We should most definitely be paying attention to those nudges as we also listen for our Father's voice! God isn't going to lead us anywhere He isn't at. The plans God has for us are good. They aren't to harm us. They are to give us a hope and a future (Jeremiah 29:11).

We don't have to resent a future season of our lives just because we are enjoying where we are at now. One huge blessing of my weekend visit to Liberty was getting to meet Emma Mae Jenkins. Our encounter and time of interaction was nothing short of a hug from God. It reminded me that God doesn't just know the desires of my heart. He acts upon them. As another girl and I shared things with Emma, she said that God wants us to enjoy where we are currently at. That doesn't sound like a big deal, but it is so true! We, as humans, are often looking for the next thing. We struggle to be content with the current second and set of circumstances we have. As I have said many times before, I am loving this school year. Because of that, I have sometimes felt guilty for not being gung-ho in thinking about dorm decorations. **God knows exactly what we need, though, my friend. He is more than enough for us. We must be willing to go where He leads us, and we must strive to have extraordinary faith in believing in what God can do. Nothing is too hard for Him.**

Nothing can stop or stand in the way of the plans God has for your life! Jesus whispered that sweet message into my spirit a few years ago and reminds me of it every day.

I also want to challenge you to believe in the power of prayer. Jesus cares about the things you care about! I have prayed for so many different things recently. I am honestly so glad God protects the conversations I have with Him near the woods! I have seen my Heavenly Father bring a new Bible Study to life in my school. He actually gave me a nudge about leading a new Bible Study a few months ago around the time of the flood. I had no clue what the details would be of what He was calling me to, but I kept praying about it. It is truly amazing to see God work! He also placed a nudge within the headmaster of my school about the Bible Study. My headmaster approached me, mentioned the possibility of starting a middle school discipleship group, and asked if I would be interested in leading it! The Lord had already warned me about His work! I had no clue He would use my headmaster to help bring this plan of His to fruition! God blessed my commitment to pray over the nudge He placed within me! I am so excited to share with you that Renew Bible Study starts this Friday! I cannot wait to spiritually invest into the lives of the girls Jesus places in my life!

Whether you are praying for a friend's hurt ankle, a special revelation from God, discernment in making decisions, or trusting God to provide the scholarships you need to pay for college, **keep praying. Believe in the power of prayer.** God is with you every step that you take! He is never going to stop pursuing you! His love for you is always raw, fresh, and new. It is never stagnant!

I pray that as we trust God to do the miraculous things in our lives, His love will be vibrant in and through us!

Let's enjoy the plans God has for our lives *one good step at a time.*

Much love,

Haley

2018: A FOCUS ON GOD'S FAITHFULNESS

DECEMBER 30, 2018

2018 has been a year of growing in ministry in deeper ways than I have ever experienced before. During snow days in January and every minute I could, I was planning the Delight Movement. God gave me a burden and passion for middle and high school girls after I was prophesied over at the United Conference in August of 2017. **It was time fear no longer gripped my speech.** My God said He was going to use my words in an even greater way than He currently was. I was humbled by the vision the Lord instilled within me.

God reminded me of His protection and the brevity of life in January. The night before my siblings and I were in a car accident, I wrote the following words in my journal: "You deserve better than my best, Lord. Please keep us close to Yourself. Keep my eyes on You so that I do not fall. I know the enemy is ticked off because of what You are doing in and through my life. I know he will try to distract me and make me fall, but, God, You are my upholder. You are my base. You keep my feet secure and firm. You give me a strong, steady, and unwavering base/balance. I am Yours, Lord. Yours alone. My life is Yours. Wherever, whenever, and whatever-I am here for You alone. Thank You for using my life, Lord. Please help me live worthy to the calling I have received from You." The enemy attempted to take my life the day after I wrote that prayer. My God protected the lives of my siblings and I as we were sideswiped on the way to school. When God is working, the enemy is too. The devil has already been defeated by our God though. Satan gets ticked off because he knows God is bringing life change and true Hope to the world through us.

Heaven is going to be more full because of the way God worked at The Delight Movement. Three more people are going to spend eternity in the place God's people dwell. That means three souls will no longer spend eternity in hell! At least three girls changed the path they were walking on and chose to give Jesus their everything again. Spirits of anxiety, fear, depression, and oppression were eradicated from the hearts and lives of God's precious daughters. I can't even imagine how many seeds God planted in His girls' lives. **The power of God within us, His children, is more powerful than we even realize!**

Helping plan my junior prom was such a special experience to me. A whole year before prom, I was praying passionately about who I would go to prom with. My Father didn't reveal His best in my prom date to me immediately. Rather, He had intense lessons to teach me during the journey. I had to recognize that only God can truly satisfy my heart. Only Jesus can bring me the joy and hope I need. After mentally crossing off the names of prom date candidates, I thought I had discovered God's best. I really thought I had finally received the answers to my prayers. Nope. After realizing my plan was not God's plan, I sought the Lord for Who He was and stopped focusing on what He could do for me. I even stopped focusing on my prom date situation. All along, I just knew that the Lord was doing something special. I was not close to any guy and really did not know how the Lord was going to work something out. I just trusted that God was doing something even though I could not see the whole plan.

After surrendering my desires to the Lord and acknowledging that He alone was more than enough for me, Jesus' beautiful plan for my prom experience unfolded. The answers to prayer I experienced on May 5, 2018 made me aware that God's plans truly are the best for us. While I was tempted to give up on the plans God gave me a heart for, He reminded me to trust Him. **The Lord's timing definitely isn't ours, but His timing is a teacher to us.** I honestly believe that Josh and I had the best night at prom because of how much I had invested prayer into it. **Prayer makes us appreciate the miracles God does for us. It opens our eyes to the details of the Lord.** After prom, the Lord even incorporated Target (one of my favorite stores) into my special night. **Jesus doesn't just know the desires of our hearts. He acts upon them.** God doesn't withhold fun from His children. He actually is the Giver of all life and every good thing. We must remind ourselves of that whenever the enemy makes us think we are missing out on fun. The "fun" of the world is evil and only leads to death. Doing things to please God and glorify Him is much more satisfying than any temporary pleasure. Let's choose Jesus over everything. He alone is the One Who satisfies our parched hearts in dry and desolate places. I beg you to cling onto Him if you are still wandering around looking for true Hope, my friend.

Our lives on earth are temporary. We don't have forever to spend here. **Every minute that we have matters.** How are you using your time? Are you making a difference for eternity, or are you wasting it on social media or false pleasures?

We must stop dreaming small. What dream has the Lord placed in your heart? What vision has He given to you? **You never know how impactful your acts of obedience will be! Trust God to do what He has promised you. Don't give up during the journey just because it is challenging.**

We will never grow if we always stay inside the walls of our comfort zones. Leaving Bethel was not my original plan at all. Oh my. I literally grew up there and knew the place like the back of my hand! Bethel (my old school) was a home to me. It was my place of doing ministry, loving my classmates, giving baked goods, and spreading encouragement. **God let me know that He had**

more people for me to impact. The work He had planned for me to do at Bethel was accomplished. I had finished that mission. There were new souls awaiting the hope and message He had to share with them through me.

Trusting God was a common theme of 2018 for me. I was clenched onto the steering wheel of my life before changing schools. I had to willingly let go of the wheel, sit in the passenger seat, and trust God to lead me in the places He wanted me to go. Not knowing what is ahead is scary to me. Yet, as I let go of control, God allowed me to have His absolute peace.

I love my new school. Some aspects of it remind me of cool schools on TV shows. I love the people I have had the privilege of getting to know. Going into the school year, I had my guard up. I honestly did not expect to make any great connections or friendships with people. I was excited about being accepted into Liberty, ready to be done with high school, and just looking forward to the future. That attitude of mine did not last long. God invaded my life with the power of vulnerability. I connected with one of my classmates, realized I played a vital role in the place God had positioned me, and sought to bring change to my sweet school. I started engaging in conversations with people I had never met before and fell in love with the authenticity of people's stories.

To be honest with you, I started to love this season of my life so much that I actually began to resent the season of college God had in store for me! Isn't that crazy? Jesus taught me balance the first few months of school. That was a talent I had not even touched on much before. He showed me that **I can enjoy the season I am currently in without resenting the seasons to come. God wants us to be saturated with Him and overflow with Him in each present moment.** He wants us to live in such a way we forget about documenting every moment with a picture. Jesus wants us to live life to the fullest while making the most eternal impact for His kingdom.

It was during Hurricane Florence that I sat on my front porch and felt the wind hurling. God had placed a phrase before me that was puzzling. I was seeking Him and asking Jesus to unfold the mystery of "Permissible and Beneficial" to me. I learned that permissible things are allowed. They may even seem good. They are okay, but beneficial things are going to give God the most glory.

While praying over an idea the Lord gave me, I really desired to make a difference in the lives of middle school girls at my school. I wanted to engage with them, know their names, do life with them, and share wisdom the Lord was revealing to me. Feeling like the Lord wanted me to lead a Bible study, I ordered a book I would use for it. I just did not know the details for the Bible study I felt called to lead. I didn't know when, where, or how it would take place. As my peers and I were preparing for our National Honor Society Induction Ceremony, my headmaster motioned for me to come talk with him. He asked if I would be interested in leading a middle school girls discipleship group! I told him I had already ordered the book for it! Isn't it amazing to see God work? I later found out that one of my teachers had been praying for a Bible study like this to happen for the past three years! **Jesus showed me that the nudges He places within us are set in motion long before we are made aware of them.** My sweet middle school girls challenge my heart and encourage me so much. Seeing the eighth grade girls step up and lead during our Renew Christmas party made my heart swell. Jonathan, one of my dear friends, recently reminded me that doing ministry involves preparing others to do the work of the Lord. We must step back and let others get their hands in the work right before us. **Loving God and loving His people are two of our greatest callings and responsibilities! We must be careful to not do life intimately with people who limit us in those two important callings.**

Renew (the name of our Bible study) was inspired by Psalm 51:10 (NIV). It is a verse I constantly have running through my mind. It states, "Create in me a pure heart, O God, and renew a steadfast spirit within me." Jesus also humbled me with Matthew 5:8 (NIV) which exclaims, "Blessed are the pure in heart, for they will see God." I long to be uncontaminated before my Father. The first lesson my Bible study discussed was the importance of filters in our lives. I told the girls that hot water is often used in removing impurities. I also challenged the girls and myself to let God filter out the impurities from our personal lives. I literally did not expect my life to be so filtered the following week, but it was. God ordained that first message and even allowed our group to outgrow our first room the first week!

Girls on the front row were sponges absorbing every word the Lord was saying through me. Girls in the middle of the room were sharing things to add to our lesson, and girls in the back were leaders as they were present and engaged as well.

I was so humbled and thankful for the way God birthed this nudge He placed within my heart. Our group has about 20 girls attend each week! Doing life with them is a privilege to me. I treasure the way they trust me with their prayer requests, and I am blown away by the wisdom they add to our lessons!

I was also supposed to do a Spanish course through Pitt Community College the first part of the school year. After applying to the program this summer, I was told the class was full. Instead of worrying about my plans falling through, God gave me peace about the situation. He knew how my schedule would be and graciously allowed me to have the first few months of school to do other things. While I am about to embark on this new Spanish course, I'm just reminded of the perfection in God's timing.

Changing schools has also provided me with help in publishing my first book! Friend, I really cannot say thank you to Jesus enough for these blessings in my life! **The things He places within us have purpose outside of us.**

Undeniably His turned three this year! The cake I made to celebrate its birthday was sloppy and hideous to say the least! I kept turning the cake platter around to avoid showing the crumbly side to my dad. Undeniably His has also reached over 34 countries in the past three years! All glory goes to God for the work He continues to do through it! **Never underestimate the work God wants to do through you. Don't lay in a box of insecurities when God has given you holy confidence to walk in and to walk through.**

After experiencing a tough circumstance in my life a month ago, the Lord gently reminded me that I'm always in need of Him and desperate for Him. **I need God just as much on my best days as I need Him on my worst days.** Jesus always makes Himself available to us. He never turns us away. Let's make sure our identities are in Him alone. Let's not get so busy that we forget that our greatest need is the **Giver** of all good things.

I love the fact that even in storms I'm not going to be shaken. That is hope that comes from having Jesus as our foundation. What is your hope in, my friend? Storms are going to come in our lives. We must be prepared for them. Preparing for things is just as important as experiencing things.

My spirit longs to see all people awakened to God's light, love, and truth! It's time for blinders to be cut and fall right on the ground. I'm tired of the enemy receiving happiness from the actions of God's people. It is time for the Lord's bride to wake up! Did you realize that as a child of God, you are God's bride? That is something I think we forget. **A relationship without communication is nonexistent.** How is your relationship with God doing? Like the story of Hosea and Gomer in the Bible, **God's love is faithful and persistent for us even**

when we are unfaithful and run away. God's heart for His people is redemption. He constantly longs to see His lost sheep return home. Do you need to return home? Don't keep listening to Satan's lies. You are never going to be enough on your own. You can't get through this battle alone. You are going to need Help. Only Jesus is strong enough to get you through this battle and journey. Cling onto Jesus, dear friend. I cannot even describe the hope and joy we experience in God. After seeking Jesus and finding Him in such intense ways, Jesus allowed me to burst forth with His joy like never before a few weeks ago. I can't even explain how evident, undeniable, and contagious the joy of the Lord is. Instead of wallowing in fear or anger over your circumstances, I challenge you to wake up, sit up, and experience the joy awaiting you in Christ Jesus alone.

If you are looking for God's peace in determining your plans, keep praying. Don't stop seeking our Father's heart. Don't give up before the blessing is revealed to you. If God has spoken a word into your spirit, keep believing it. Don't give up. There is Hope.

You can still sing, dance, love, care for people, and love people no matter who is given or taken away from your life. Make the most of the seasons you have with people you hold dear. Don't miss a minute or opportunity you are supposed to spend with them. Pray for your people. Show them Jesus' authentic and pure love. Never stop letting them know that you care about them. **Realize that not all people are meant to be in your life forever though, my friend. In all things, trust that God is going to use your pain for a great purpose.** He hasn't left us as orphans (John 14:18). **Every step that God has for us is good. And, believe me, God always has a good next step for us to take.** There is always more in the Lord. His plans are never less. They are immeasurably more than our wildest hopes, dreams, and plans (Ephesians 3:20).

What story has God written throughout the pages of your life this year, brother or sister? Is it a story you are proud to share? If so, share your story so that you can give God most glory. I love how 1 Timothy 4:15 (NIV) states, "Be diligent in these matters; give yourself wholly to them, so that everyone may see your progress." **Your progress matters.** Never think that it doesn't. **If your story is one that you are embarrassed of, know that God can make your story new. He will use the wounds and hurts from your past to share His story of hope through your scars.** Don't look to a new year to fulfill your longings. Don't look for a new relationship or haircut to satisfy you either. God formed you and created you on purpose for a purpose. He knit you together in your mother's womb (Psalm 139:13).

Let's be bold in the days to come, my friend. I want to embrace the people God places in my path. I want to be excited and expectant in the Lord, not underestimating what He can do for me. If I have learned anything this year, I have learned to trust God's plans and to trust His timing of them. We must keep seeking our Father's heart. Let's not forget to be still in His Presence and just seek Him as our Lover and Best Friend. Let's share our hearts with the Lord and go on many walks and talks with Him.

I am bursting forth with joy for all the Lord has done in my life this year, and I am pouring out praise for the miracles I have witnessed. My God is faithful always.

A verse I have clung onto this year is Galatians 6:9 (NIV). Tuck it in the pocket of your heart and be reminded of it. **"Let us not become weary in doing good, for at the proper time we will reap a harvest if we do not give up."**

NOTES

2016

1. Kupecky, Kyle and Kelsey. *The Chase*. Revell, 2015.

2017

1. Bethke, Jefferson. *It's Not What You Think*. Nelson Books, 2015.

2. Robertson, John Luke. *Young & Beardless*. Tommy Nelson. 2016.

3. Batterson, Mark. *Draw the Circle*. Zondervan, 2012.

2018

1. Goff, Bob. *Love Does*. Nelson Books, 2012.

2. Batterson, Mark. *The Circle Maker*. Zondervan, 2011.

Acknowledgments

TO MY DAD

Thank you for always challenging me to think things through, put action towards accomplishing my goals, and showing people love in unexpected ways. You are the most hardworking man I know. I admire the way you give of yourself to provide for our family. Thank you for supporting me in the things God calls me to do.

TO MY MOM

You have taught me so many of the things I know today. Thank you for cheering me on and fulfilling your God-given roles in our home. You are a woman of prayer and selfless in all you do. I'll always remember our fun days and raw conversations together.

TO MY SISTER

Thank you for always being understanding. I'm proud of who you are in Christ. I can't wait to see how He continues to grow you. You will forever be my first best friend.

TO MY BROTHER

You are gifted in extraordinary ways, little brother. Thank you for challenging my patience and bringing unique perspectives to my attention. I love you.

TO MY PASTORS, TEACHERS, AND MENTORS

Thank you for seeing things within me before I ever saw them in myself. Thank you for welcoming me in, giving me opportunities to lead, and helping me grow in my gifts. I wouldn't be where I am at today without you. I appreciate you investing your time and energy into leading me spiritually. I pray your impact on my life is multiplied and shared through my encounters with other people.

TO MY CLASSMATES

I know God has woven each of you into my life for certain seasons and reasons. My heart has been deeply burdened for you, and I hope you see Jesus through me in a pure way.

TO MY FRIENDS WHO ARE LIVING FOR JESUS WHOLEHEARTEDLY

Thank you for being pure in your devotion to Jesus Christ. Thank you for choosing Light over darkness. You radiate with peace. Your posture is different. It is rare, convicting, and inspiring. I'm forever thankful for the ways God intersected our lives. You push me closer to our Father's heart. I'm reminded to live intentionally as a result of our interactions. Never stop pursuing Jesus. Your life is more influential than you even realize. I am forever grateful for you being in mine.

TO MRS. STROUD AND MRS. BRADSHER

This project would not have been as smooth without you. Thank you for not being selfish with your knowledge from past experiences. Thank you for showing humility and choosing to help me. You will never know how blessed I have felt by being encouraged by you in this journey. I hope to be just as giving to others as you have been to me. Thank you so much for choosing to invest into me.

TO EVERYONE WHO HAS LOVED AND ENCOURAGED ME

Thank you. Thank you for praying for me, embracing me, and supporting me in the ministries God has laid on my heart. Your sweet comments and gentle words have helped bring confirmation to the callings God has spoken over me. I pray your spirit is blessed by this book as you continue to love and encourage all those you meet.

TO MY VERY BEST FRIEND, SAVIOR, AND LORD

My words can't express Your glory and splendor. My favorite place to be is with You in the woods. Thank You for listening to me and never turning me away. You rid me of pressures and overwhelm me with indescribable peace. I'm beyond grateful for our journey together. You are indeed faithful. You are most creative, and I will never be able to understand Your immense love. Thank You for rescuing me. Thank You for protecting me from the enemy's traps. Thank You for revealing Yourself to me in intimate ways. I'm confident in You, knowing I will never walk alone. Thank You for leading my life and not letting me miss out on anything You have in store for me. You are my everything, and with You I lack no good thing. Use my life in bigger ways than I could ever imagine. Keep me fully consecrated and devoted to You. *Fully Consecrated* exists because of You. Thank You for planting seeds in the hearts and lives of Your children. Thank You for growing this dream within me and for birthing it through me. I am in awe of the way You work. Thank You for choosing to use little me to accomplish Your great tasks. I pray this book brings You more glory. I pray it opens people's eyes to see how real You are. I pray Heaven is more full because of this journey we have had together. Thank You for doing immeasurably more than I could ever imagine. My life is Yours and so is this book. Thank you for being the Writer. You deserve the glory and every inch of praise. I love You, Abba. This is just the beginning of some even more beautiful things You have in store.

ABOUT THE AUTHOR

Undeniably His is one of the platforms Haley Wade has been given to share the messages God lays on her heart. Haley is currently growing in her biblical leadership skills as she leads a middle school girls Bible study at her school.

Haley longs to represent Jesus purely, use her gifts to point others to Christ, and serve others in a humble way.

As Haley will soon embark on an adventure after high school, she is trusting in God with the things unseen. Haley feels called to use her words, expressions of encouragement, and passionate creativity to make Heaven more full for eternity. She is also excited and expectant to see the ways God continues to work in, through, and around her in the future.

Connect with Haley on her blog

UNDENIABLYHIS.COM

AN EXPLANATION OF THE GOSPEL

BY ALEX HAYS

"For God so loved the world that he gave his one and only Son, that whoever believes in him shall not perish but have eternal life." -John 3:16 (NIV)

For God so loved the world— this statement first marks the relationship between God and man.

The God of the universe, the God who hung the stars in the night sky and causes the sun to rise and set, is madly in love with you. His love is so deep and intricate that it stretches from the beginning to the end of time. He was willing to go to any length to ransom you. His plan for our rescue, redemption, and restoration was formed before the foundations of the world were laid. He wanted to save us so desperately from the sin that so easily entangles every one of us that He was willing to descend from the glory of the heavens and make Himself like us and walk among us.

He came to us as a man named Jesus. Born from a virgin, He lived a perfect and blameless life. He took all of our guilt and shame upon Himself so that HE could pay the debt that WE owed. Jesus was crucified on a cross at Calvary. Jesus gave Himself for us all because of His love towards us while we were still sinners (Romans 5:8). He came not to condemn us, but to save us that we may be righteous and stand before God clean and blameless covered under His blood. Jesus gave Himself not because of what we have done or can do, but because of what He has already done for us.

A Christian is more than just a label. It is a life-changing and soul-transforming experience. To become a Christian is to live our lives in faith and in obedience to His Word trusting that through His victory, we are restored and forgiven.

You may feel that you have gone too far or that your sins are too great. But there is a God who loves you unconditionally. He is eagerly waiting for you with open arms. If you can feel the tugging on your heart for you to make things right with God, right now seek the Lord with a humble heart. Ask Him to forgive you and come into your life. Ask Him for a new heart that seeks and longs for righteousness and truth. He is always faithful to forgive and restore all those who come to Him with an honest and open heart.

"What can wash away my sin? Nothing but the blood of Jesus."

Lowry, Robert. "Nothing but the Blood of Jesus." 1876.

Alex Hays is a young and dedicated evangelist whose soul is set on fire by the Word of God and the power of the Holy Spirit. After having an incredible encounter with God in 2017, he began his ministry at the age of 19. Alex has preached in many revivals since the start of his ministry. He preaches with passion, fire, and a desire to see an outpouring of the Holy Ghost! Alex's sole purpose in this life is to give testimony and bear witness to the redeeming power of the blood of Jesus Christ and the power that was displayed on the cross at Calvary.

Have you embarked on a journey of recognizing God's faithfulness in your life, my friend? Have you opened up your heart to the plans God has in store for you? This life on earth is temporary, but we will live for eternity. Where are you going to spend yours?

www.ingramcontent.com/pod-product-compliance
Lightning Source LLC
Chambersburg PA
CBHW081221170426
43198CB00017B/2676